PRAISE FOR *SECRET'S OF A SECRET SHOPPER*

Greg's ministry provided a really valuable perspective on our weekend experiences as a church. His heart for the Kingdom and passion to see every church reach its maximum potential is a gift to those of us who care deeply about seeing our churches thrive.

- John Ortberg, Senior Pastor, Menlo Church, Menlo Park, CA

Wow! Greg! You just greatly helped our church—again. A few years ago, when we were in a fast growing church plant, we consulted with Greg as a secret shopper. His insight changed our church. He forced us to think about things we hadn't considered. It was hugely helpful. Today, as I pastor an established church, we've still incorporated some of those same ideas. Now we have a handbook for further discovery and improvement. What a valuable resource for the church and Kingdom! Thanks Greg.

- Ron Edmondson, Pastor and Leadership Consultant

Your church has secret shoppers every Sunday. The problem is . . . you don't know who they are because they visit and never return. Greg Atkinson is giving your ministry GOLD with his new book *Secrets of a Secret Shopper.* If you want to know what people really think and experience when they visit your church, then you—*and your entire* team—need to read this book.

- Jenni Catron, Leadership Consultant and Author
of *The 4 Dimensions of Extraordinary Leadership*

Greg Atkinson has given us a fast read that is a must read. Church leaders work so hard to get people to come to church, and then wonder why they don't return. Greg's practical insights are based on proven experience that help you see what you might miss on your own. The secret shopper process will help you improve your overall church experience from the parking lot to the altar!

- Dan Reiland, Executive Pastor, 12Stone Church, Lawrenceville, GA

The way you feel about a guest coming in your church will be directly reflected in how they feel about you when they walk out of your church. You no longer have to just imagine what a great experience could feel like for a guest. Help is here in *Secrets of a Secret Shopper*. Why not intentionally create a remarkable guest experience that results in them coming back and bringing someone with them? Greg shares his secrets to help churches create moments of surprise and delight.

- **Jason Young, Director of Guest Services, North Point Ministries**

If you're going to care well for new guests at your church, then you must care about the things your guests care about when they arrive. Consider this book a gift. It's the report of a secret shopper that serves as your "heads up" before the secret shopper arrives. This resource from Greg is full of practical, tangible, and detailed applications that will equip you and your teams to communicate God's love to the people arriving at your church. Read it. Study it. Share it. And apply it. Your guests will thank you.

- **Mark Waltz, Executive Pastor, Granger Community Church, Author of *First Impressions***

Successful corporations have for years put a premium of understanding what a guest experiences. The dirty secret with most churches is we are clueless. We evaluate the sermon, but reaching people far from Jesus takes more than a catchy 30-minute message. If you want to know how to evaluate what someone experiences the time they look up your church in our digital age to the time they leave your parking lot, start reading now!

- Ashley Wooldridge, Executive Pastor, Christ's Church of the Valley, Phoenix, AZ

Greg Atkinson has been called to help build the church and truly desires to see every local church maximize its ministry. Greg will help you make sure you are doing everything possible to reach as many as possible for Jesus Christ.

- Ben Lovvorn, Executive Pastor of Operations, First Baptist Dallas

SECRETS OF A SECRET SHOPPER

REACHING AND KEEPING CHURCH GUESTS

GREG ATKINSON

Published by Rainer Publishing
www.RainerPublishing.com

ISBN 978-0-9978861-3-9

Printed in the United States of America

DEDICATION

I dedicate this book to the memory of my friend and mentor Billy Hornsby. Billy was a great and godly man who taught me much about God, life, joy, and a passion for church planting.

Especially important to this book is the fact that it was Billy's idea for me to become a secret shopper. He suggested it, encouraged me, and then gave me my first endorsement. Billy went out of his way to tell churches about my ministry and encourage them to bring me in.

I will always treasure our time together and will never forget what a loving husband, father, and grandfather he was. The way he loved his dear wife, Charlene, leaves a lasting impression on me and that's what this book is ultimately about—leaving a lasting impression.

I look forward to the day when I laugh with Billy and Charlene again in heaven.

ACKNOWLEDGMENTS

I'd like to thank my family for believing in me and encouraging me to write. As usual, my wife is my first editor and a dear partner in ministry.

I'd like to thank all the churches over the years that have brought me in to consult or do a secret shopper visit. Without your investment in my ministry and your dedication to be better at what you do, I would not have anything to write about.

Once again, I'm grateful to partner with my friends at Rainer Publishing and am thankful for our partnership to encourage, equip, and train pastors. To God be all glory for how He uses this book and how He continues to build His church.

CONTENTS

FOREWORD

The top priority for us at Bayside is to take great care of everyone God sends to us. So let me ask you a question: When was the last time you visited a church for the first-time? Maybe you've been a part of the same church for your entire life. But if you've gone to visit a friend, or a child or grandchild or maybe even just visited a church while on vacation, you know the nerves and uneasiness that goes along with it.

At Bayside we have a Guest Services Team, and it is their mission to help that first visit be as smooth and as welcoming as possible. We like to surprise people by exceeding their expectations.

As a multisite church in an increasingly post-Christian culture on the West Coast, we are constantly seeking to improve in this area. We know you only get one chance to make a positive first impression, so we train our people, cast vision, and bring in someone like Greg Atkinson to show us where we are weak and point out things we weren't aware of.

Greg Atkinson is smart, detailed, and thorough. He saw things that we would never notice. His feedback was invaluable and we made several strategic changes as a result of his visit.

This book is a gift to the church. Greg said God laid it on his heart to write down what he looks for when he does a secret shopper visit for large churches. This book is for the benefit of the majority of churches that can't afford to invest in a service like this, or maybe are a little skeptical.

If you're skeptical, unsure of the value of a secret shopper, or maybe have never considered how crucial first impressions can be to a church, this book is for you. In this book are the things or "secrets" that churches pay Greg to look for.

Read it twice. Make strategic and intentional changes. Train your staff, your leaders, and your volunteers to be ready for guests and to as Greg says, "Kill them with kindness."

Thank you Greg for your desire to see every church reach and keep more guests for the glory of God.

Ray Johnston
Founding & Lead Pastor
Bayside Church
www.rayjohnston.com

INTRODUCTION

When you think of churches doing an excellent job with hospitality, what comes to mind? Pristine bathrooms? Friendly greeters? Knowledgeable parking attendants? Secure children's environments? Yes, each of these areas is part of being hospitable. Every church should focus on them. But the true meaning and practice of hospitality goes much deeper than a checklist of actions or areas of responsibility. In fact, the practice of true hospitality can be eternity-altering.

Somehow we've missed the biblical definition of the word. In the Greek, "hospitality" is written φιλόξενος—a combination of two distinct words and concepts. The word φιλό (pronounced *philao*) is one of several meaning "love," but in this case it means brotherly love. The word ξενος (*xenos*) makes up the second half of the Greek term, and it means "stranger."

When the two terms and their definitions are combined into

one term, translated *philoxenia*, we see that hospitality literally means "showing brotherly love to strangers." How does knowing this biblical definition impact how we read the numerous scriptures throughout the Old and New Testament that reference hospitality? What does this new application mean for us as church leaders?

A BIBLICAL MANDATE

While hospitality may sometimes be perceived as a unique gifting for some people, Scripture is clear that loving strangers is a biblical mandate to *anyone* who follows Jesus. Throughout the Old Testament, God specifically commands His people to practice hospitality. In Leviticus 19:33-34, He tells the Israelites to "love the stranger" like they love themselves—reminding them that they, too, were once strangers:

> *"When a stranger sojourns with you in your land, you shall not do him wrong. You shall treat the stranger who sojourns with you as the native among you, you shall love him as yourself, for you were strangers in the land of Egypt. I am the LORD your God." (Leviticus 19:33-34 ESV).*

Some 400 years later in the gospel of Matthew, Jesus talks about the hospitable behavior of those who will inherit the Kingdom: "For I was hungry and you gave Me something to eat; I was thirsty, and you gave Me something to drink; I was a stranger, and you invited Me in; naked, and you clothed Me; I was sick, and you visited me; I was in prison, and you came to Me." (Matt. 25:34-36 NASB). When we welcome the least of these and treat them as valued guests, we welcome Christ Himself. And like so much of 1 John shows us, when we love others, we show our love for God. Hospitality is also a specific hallmark for church leaders. In 1 Timothy 3:2 and Titus 1:7-8, Paul lays out important guidelines and criteria for church leadership, he tells the leaders of the church that they must be known for being hospitable.

With the command to practice the loving of strangers so prevalent throughout Scripture, it seems that showing hospitality is one of the primary signs of a follower of Jesus—and a church that follows Jesus. In fact, Jesus says that by loving others, others will know we are His disciples (John 13:35).

A HOSPITALITY-PRACTICING CHURCH

Perhaps one of the most grace-filled examples of hospitality in the Old Testament is the system that God sets up allowing all people—both rich and poor—to approach the tabernacle and offer sacrifices to Him for their forgiveness. Via this system, travelers could come to the temple to offer sacrifices and worship God. No one's economic status excluded them.

In the same way, because of Jesus' sacrifice on the cross for our sins, we are able and welcome to come to Him. Everyone—including those who don't yet know God—should be able and welcome to come to His Church, which Paul calls "God's household" (1 Tim. 3:15). When we welcome strangers into our church and show love to them, we emulate His love and compassion—the same hospitality He showed to us as He welcomed us as "foreigners and strangers" and made us "members of His household" (Eph. 2:19-20). A church that welcomes strangers and practices true hospitality is a living, breathing community where God dwells.

Are you leading a church that loves strangers? Would your surrounding community say you are a church of love and compassion where *anyone* would feel welcome? Do the hearts and attitudes—not just actions—of your people reflect a true desire to bring others into God's household? As we begin to see the loving of strangers as fundamental to the life and heart of the church, my prayer is that our churches would gain a greater vision of hospitality and that by practicing the loving of strangers we would become churches where true transformation happens and eternities are altered.

THE CHURCH SECRET SHOPPER

So why are there church secret shoppers? Are we trying to cater to consumers or teach church leaders how to entertain? Certainly not. I can't speak for all secret shoppers, but for myself and my friends that I know, we take seriously welcoming "strangers" or guests into our weekly worship experience. We know it matters, and I want to help you do it better. That's why I'm writing this book. In particular, I'm writing this book to pastors that lead a small to mid-sized congregation. Many churches this size do not have the financial capabilities to hire consultants. Through this book, I want to help you make strategic changes to your church's guest experience.

Imagine you're hosting a small group in your home. Imagine you're hosting a birthday party. Imagine you're having friends over for dinner. Can you picture one of these scenarios? When you have company over, what do you do? You clean house! You prepare. You want to welcome your company with open arms and make sure they feel right at home. This is what this book is about. Every week thousands of guests visit our local churches. We need to clean house, prepare, and be ready to host them.

All of us need to have the mindset and expectation that company is coming. How we prepare for and welcome "company" or guests to our churches says a lot about how seriously we take the Great Commission. There's a reason churches have changed their ministry title from First Impressions to Guest Services or Hospitality. At my church, we have a hospitality team. We want our people to be loved and taken care of. From young to old, you are special in God's eyes, and you're special and valued to us as ministers of the gospel. So, I've laid the groundwork, and now it's time to begin. Company is coming. Are you ready?

> Taste and see that the LORD is good.
>
> – Psalm 34:8 (NLT)

One of my greatest passions is leadership. If you're familiar with my previous books, you know I have a heart for leaders, especially church leaders and pastors. I write books to help equip them and coach them on how to do what they do better. Is it because I know it all? Most definitely not! It's because after two decades of ministry experience, lots of consulting with churches of all sizes around the country, and speaking at conferences and training thousands of church leaders around the world, I have picked up a thing or two about leadership, especially as it relates to leading a church. I also ask a lot of questions and have learned a great deal from other leaders far wiser and more gifted than me.

Let me say up front that I knew when I announced that I was writing this book that it would be controversial. Some people have always been opposed to me operating as a secret shopper. They say, "Just preach the Word and you'll be fine." I'm all for "preaching the Word," but I think if we are going to open our church doors up to the public and invite outsiders in, we need to expect people are going to critique us. Those not familiar with the church have built-in barriers to church, Christians, and worship. We need to help them overcome these barriers.

I also know that when I write a book like this that many think this is to appeal to the consumeristic side of North American Christianity. You may assume, unfairly so, that this book is about keeping people happy and is therefore not biblical. I assure you that I've not gone off the deep end and am not into people pleasing. I am, however, into tearing down walls, barriers, and obstacles. As Andy Stanley shared in his book *Deep and Wide*, he loves this verse in Scripture:

"It is my judgment, therefore, that we should not make it difficult for the Gentiles who are turning to God." – Acts 15:19 (NIV)

I love that verse too. In fact, it is what drives the writing of this book. In *Deep and Wide*, Andy Stanley writes, "From day one, I've had critics. I'm fine with that. All my critics are religious people. (It may be the only thing I have in common with Jesus.) We are unapologetically attractional. In our search for common ground with unchurched people, we've discovered that, like us, they are consumers. So we leverage their consumer instincts. By the way, if your church has heating and air conditioning, you do too.

When you read the Gospels, it's hard to overlook the fact that Jesus attracted large crowds everywhere he went. He was constantly playing to the consumer instincts of his crowds. Let's face it: It wasn't the content of his messages that appealed to the masses. Most of the time they didn't even understand what he was talking about. Heck, we're not always sure what he was talking about. People flocked to Jesus because he fed them, healed them, comforted them, and promised them things. Besides, what's the opposite of attractional? Missional? I don't think so."[1]

Speaking of attractional *vs.* missional, as I wrote in my first book *Church Leadership Essentials*, they are not opposites. They are a tension that needs to be embraced and balanced. Every church where I've served has deployed an attraction yet also missional model. I think it's a both/and thing, and even if your church is unapologetically attractional, I'd encourage your people to live life "on mission." Many churches have a core value of excellence and that is what this book is about—creating corporate weekend worship experiences that are carried out with excellence.

This book is for the churches that meet in a corporate gathering and open their doors (whether it be a church building, school, movie theater, or leased building) to the public. If you're going to invite people to your church meeting place, I want you to do things with excellence. Not to please people, but to remove barriers that could turn someone away from a chance to hear the good news.

Alan Hirsch, when writing about the attractional church wrote the following:

> "God's gracious involvement aside, if you wish to grow a contemporary church following good church growth principles, there are several things you must do and constantly improve upon:
>
> • Expand the building to allow for growth and redesign it along lines indicated in the diagram above (contemporary church-growth model).
>
> • Ensure excellent preaching in contemporary style

dealing with subjects that relate to the life of the hearers.

- Develop an inspiring worship experience (here limited to 'praise and worship) by having an excellent band and positive worship leaders.

- Make certain you have excellent parking facilities, with car park attendants, to ensure minimum inconvenience in finding a parking space.

- Ensure excellent programs in the critical area of children's and youth ministry. Do so and people will put up with less elsewhere in the mix.

- Develop a good program of cell groups built around a Christian education model to ensure pastoral care and a sense of community.

- Make sure that next week is better than last week, to keep the people coming.

This is what church-growth practitioners call the 'ministry mix.' Improvement in one area benefits the whole, and constant attention to elements of the mix will ensure growth and maximize impact. The problem is that it caters right into consumerism. And the church with the best programs and the 'sexiest' appeal tends to get more customers."[2]

I agree with the bullet points that Hirsch lists. Those are good things to do, though I don't buy into the last bullet point of making sure that the next week is better than the last. I gave up on that a long time ago. I want people to feel loved, welcomed, and wanted. I also want to remove any barriers or distractions that could keep guests from wanting to return and have a chance to hear the preaching of the gospel, or get plugged into a small group where they hear the good news.

Ben Reed, in his book *Starting Small*, wrote about the preparation that goes into Sunday morning: "Without relational connection, the church isn't the church. The church isn't a building to be occupied by people once a week. You don't believe that, and neither do I. The church is us, the people. We are the ones for whom Christ died. Not our buildings. Not our hymnals. Not our pews. It's the people who are the church. And without relational connection, you don't have a church.[3]

I wholeheartedly agree with him. When I was speaking, writing, and consulting full-time during 2014, I attended a church plant on Sunday morning and a small house church on Sunday night. The house church was a missional community. There was no production, no bulletins, no website, no greeters—just a few families that met in someone's home. You can have "church" in a number of ways. I've always said it takes all kinds of churches to reach all kinds of people. This book is for the churches and church leaders whose method and strategy and philosophy is more conventional and attractional in nature.

I'll never forget when I first heard of the website Church-MarketingSucks.com (CMS). I laughed out loud. The name instantly "clicked" with me and I knew these guys were a God-send. I once asked Brad Abare, Founder of CMS, what led to the creation of the website. He replied, "The idea for Church Marketing Sucks and The Center for Church Communication was born out of a desire to help churches get better at communication," Brad said, "Not for the sake of getting more butts in pews, but for the sake of getting more of Christ into hearts. If we really believe we have the greatest story ever told, we have got to do a better job at communicating it. The story doesn't need help, we do."

Did you catch that? It's not about getting butts in seats. It's about getting Christ into hearts. This book is about what I look for when I do a secret shopper visit for a church (regardless of church size). I've worked with small church plants, all the way to giga-churches of 20,000 attendees. I wrote this book to help you improve based on the practical tips and advice I give in these secret shopper consults, without me actually having to be there in person. I love helping churches reach more people and keep more people.

So many churches don't expect guests to visit their services and programming each week. They don't prepare, and it shows. In this book we're going to explore (in great detail) exactly what to do to prepare for newcomers. Want to know my heart and why I took the time and had the passion to write this book? Geoff Surratt, summed it up in his book *The Effective Church*:

> "The first time attender shows up a few minutes after the website said your services start because they want to sneak in the back, but when they arrive the band wasn't even on stage. The auditorium is almost empty when they sit down, which makes it easy for the pastor to find them. He explains the congregation is notoriously late, but the service will start in a few minutes.

During service the guest notices that the words are wrong on some of the slides, and there are several typos in the bulletin. On the way out to the car they notice the pile of junk on a table in the corner, seemingly the same pile of junk that was there when they visited last Christmas. In the parking lot the overgrown flower beds seems to emphasize the message, 'We do the least we can.'

The new attender can't help but wonder why the church leaders care so little about details. Maybe that's the way they treat people as well? It's not really worth the effort to find out."[4]

This, my friends, is what this book is about—all the details. It's about leading and serving with excellence. Not only that, it's about a mentality. When training hospitality team members, I always coach them to "kill them with kindness." I share the example of Chick-fil-A and how they always have excellent customer service. Whenever I thank an employee for going out of the way for me, they always respond with, "my pleasure." Wow! What an impression. What a dining experience, especially for fast food. This is what I mean by "kill them with kindness" and the mentality we have to have when dealing with people, especially guests that visit our churches.

Andy Stanley writes, "We must remove every possible obstacle from the path of the disinterested, suspicious, here-against-my-will, would-rather-be-somewhere-else, unchurched guests. The parking lot, hallways, auditorium, and stage must be obstacle-free zones."[5]

I agree, and I'd like to help you do that. I mentioned at the beginning of the Introduction that I love leadership. As you well know, leaders are servants first. This is my way of serving you and the big "C" Church. So, dear pastor, if you want to do whatever it takes to reach those far from God and remove distractions, then you've picked up the right book. Let's dive in!

1
ONLINE PRESENCE

Why is the first chapter of this book on online presence? Because when I do a secret shopper for a church, the first thing I evaluate is their online presence. I have checked them out online before I ever arrive at their church, just like people in your city do. Burn these words into your brain: Guests will visit you online before they visit you in person. Count on it. You wouldn't believe how many churches across the country ignore or don't take seriously their online presence. What do I mean by online presence? I'm talking about your church's website and use of social media (Facebook, Twitter, You-Tube, Instagram, Google, Vine, Bing, Podcasts, etc.).

I can't stress this enough: Your church's online presence is the front door of your church. It has been said that people now visit your church up to ten times before they physically attend a worship service. Your first impression as a church is on social media. Your second impression is your mobile site. Your third impression is your church website. Your next impression is the parking lot/parking team (or lack of).

The Order of First Impressions:

1. Social Media

2. Mobile Site

3. Church Website

4. Parking Lot

FACEBOOK

If Facebook was a country, it would be the world's third largest country. To think like a missionary (a digital missionary), and go where the people are, is to be present, alive, active, and engaging on Facebook. In 2008, Chris Forbes published the book *Facebook for Pastors*, in which I wrote the Foreword. In my Foreword, I made the case that all pastors should be on Facebook. Here are the reasons I gave to have a Facebook presence as a church leader or pastor:

- Being a member of Facebook allows you to be accessible.
- Being a member of Facebook is in line with a kingdom focus.
- Being a member of Facebook shows that we're all human.
- Being a member of Facebook gives others a look at your heart and passions.
- Being a member of Facebook encourages learning, sharing, and discussion.
- Facebook is another door into your local church.

I want to focus on that last point as it relates to your church corporately. All around your local church are people that need to know God. I'd wager that most of them are on Facebook and are friends with people in your congregation. Maybe they're related to them. Maybe they grew up or went to school with them. Maybe they work with them. The point is somehow they know people in your church. When your church members are active on Facebook and like and share things from your church's Facebook page, it has impact on those in their circle of influence.

As a campus pastor, I have used Facebook extensively to reach out into our community and raise awareness of what we were doing as a congregation. I can't stress enough how crucial it is for you as a pastor or church leader, as well as your congregation, to be active and engaging on social media, particularly Facebook.

What do I mean by engaging? It means to not just post announcements and events on your church's Facebook pages, but to seek to interact and engage in conversation. Ask questions. Encourage feedback and comments. Don't just be a broadcast tool. The following excerpt is from Bill Seaver's MicroExplosion blog from January 7, 2009:

> "A lot of companies are considering trying some new marketing approaches these days. They have become enamored or curious about the new social media tools that are widely publicized and are trying to determine how it can work for them. This is a good spot to be in, but I've realized something is still missing. What's missing is the appropriate mindset needed to use the social media tools, techniques, and strategies well. **The old mindset won't work with the new tools. They don't mix.** Seth Godin wrote an entire book about that called Meatball Sundae.
>
> New marketing only works with the new mindset. Simply using the new tools with the old mindset won't

bring about the marketing results you need and want."[6]

I know what some of you are thinking. This is going to take time. It's less than you may think. First of all, you don't have to be the one posting to the church's Facebook page. You can have a volunteer or staff member handle your church's Facebook page. I'd say to post one or two times a day. Again, always encourage interaction. I'm willing to bet there is a volunteer or servant leader in your congregation that would love to champion this for your church. Here are some Facebook tips from Nils Smith:

> "When it comes to your church Facebook page many churches are finding that no one is seeing any of their posts. The problem though isn't always Facebook as much as it is what you are saying. I continue to work with many churches and ministries that are growing tremendously on Facebook without any advertising (although ads do help significantly). Here are 4 types of posts that I recommend you using as a part of your content strategy:

1. Inspiration - at least 50% of your posts should be inspirational. This should include sermon video clips or quotes,

Bible verses, inspirational messages or images, etc. Ask yourself when posting: will someone Like or Share this?

2. Information - too many churches post informational posts as 100% of their strategy. At most it should be 25%, but it also shouldn't be 0%. People need to know what's going on and how and where they can get connected.

3. Conversation - Dave Adamson recently said that at North Point Church they strive to use more questions marks than periods. Facebook is a social network, which means that conversation is central to the platform and the best way to create a conversation is to ask a question.

4. Celebration - tell more stories! It sounds simple, but we focus more on our what God has ahead and too often don't take time to pause and look at all that God has done. Whether it's a ministry highlight or a personal testimony, capturing and sharing stories is critically valuable to your Facebook page content."[7]

As you get going, know that you have never landed. What worked this year will likely not work next year. The point is to make Facebook a priority. Or if you're reading these words five years from the time this book is published and another social media platform is where everyone congregates, be present and active there.

TWITTER AND INSTAGRAM

As for Twitter and Instagram (and Snapchat for some churches), you've got to know your people. If you're a rural church, probably most of your people aren't on Twitter. With Twitter and Instagram, seek to have more engagement. Post picture quotes and sharable content that others can like and share. Pictures are great on both Twitter and Instagram. On Instagram and Snapchat, you have a wonderful opportunity to show quick video highlights or announcements.

MOBILE

A few years ago, experts predicted the rise of mobile platforms. The future is here now. Every time you sit down to eat at a restaurant, the people around you pull out their cell phones and place them on the table. We, as Americans (and even globally), are connected to others through email, the web, and apps via our mobile phones.

Why is mobile ahead of your church website in the order of first impressions? Because mobile is everywhere and people will probably check you out on their phone or tablet before they do their computer. To put this in perspective, *TIME* magazine noted on March 25 of 2013, that, "Out of the world's estimated 7 billion people, 6 billion have access to mobile phones. Far fewer — only 4.5 billion people — have access to working toilets."[8]

I will admit this is new for the church, but I think a church of any size should pay close attention to how their church website looks on a mobile device. The key to a good mobile site is "less is more." You only want the basics on your mobile site: Church name/logo, service times, directions, phone number, and maybe an About Us section.

The standard now is for a website to be responsive. What's that? When a website is *responsive*, the layout responds (or, adapts) based on the size of the screen it's presented on. A responsive website automatically changes to fit the device you're reading it on (including your mobile phone).

"If visitors see the same thing today that they saw yesterday, they probably won't visit again tomorrow."- Tony Morgan

---

WEBSITE

According to the Internet World Stats Usage and Population Statistics, 3.3 billion people (or 46.4% of the world's population) access the Internet (these are the results at the end of 2015).[9] This is huge! As a digital missionary, you have to go where the people are, and you have to be effective. In order to reach more people, you have to *invest* in a sharply designed website.

Gone are the days of a static, out-of-date website that looks like you threw it together. Gone are the days of out-of-date announcements and events that never got taken down after the event was over. Gone are the days of flash and splash pages. Gone are the days of a picture of your building or facility being the first thing a visitor sees on your homepage. People expect more. I want to push us to admit where we have created obstacles.

The following paragraph applies primarily to the technologically addicted North American culture in which you serve. I need to be brutally honest with you. The Bible says to speak the truth in love, so I'm hoping you feel the love as I hit you with some hard truth. If you're a church that meets in a church building, movie theater, school auditorium, etc. (not a house church), and you don't *invest* in a quality website, you might as well close up shop and call it quits. Did that sting? Sorry. Did that offend you? I hope not, because that is not my intent. My intent is to exhort you, challenge you, and stretch you.

As pastors, we encourage our people to intercede, invest, and invite. I'm all for your people building healthy relationships and inviting their friends, neighbors, classmates, and co-workers to church. But mark my words. Before they walk into the doors of your church, they will have already checked you out online. If they don't like what they see, then they likely won't come.

I mean we do all have the same goal and the same mission, right? We're trying to reach people far from God with the good news of the gospel and make disciples. That's our mission. In order to reach people far from God, we must think and act like missionaries. We must adapt to their culture and speak their language. Today's spiritual seeker is visual and technologically savvy. They spend an enormous amount of time online.

Please understand what I am and am not talking about. I've

worshiped in third world countries around the world. I know that God can move and be worshiped in a variety of ways. This book is addressing churches in North America in the 21st Century. Let me give you a few practical tips about your church's website:

- Clean, vibrant, responsive design is key. I know some pastors and church planters that are also graphic and web designers, and they make killer websites. Most pastors, however, don't have this in their tool belt and need to outsource the design to a professional. You can have input into the content of the website, but let a professional design it and choose the look and feel of your website. From a design standpoint, less is more.
- Decide who the website is for. At my last church (when we were designing the website), we catered it to guests with the knowledge that our attenders and members would use it too. I like when churches have an "I'm New" or "What to Expect" button on the homepage that leads to a page that answers key questions guests have when considering visiting your church.
- Make the service times and directions easy to find and highly visible.
- If your church is multisite, make the "Locations" button

or page highly visible.

- At the top or bottom of your homepage, link to the social media accounts your church uses to reach its intended community or demographic. This is a good way to get people plugged into you on social media.

- Post your sermon messages online. This could be audio only or audio and video, but your people and others considering a visit want to experience your messages.

- Also consider this point from the July/Aug 2010 *Collide* magazine article "7 Most Visited Church Website Pages": "Since your leadership or staff page is the most visited page on your church's website, you must put some thought and creativity into it. I encourage a headshot and brief bio for each staff member, along with contact info (email and phone number). Some churches do fun stuff, like interesting facts, favorite movies, books or music, etc. Make it interesting because it may be the reason someone does or does not visit your church."[10]

Hear my heart. If you're going to do something, do it with excellence. Either have a good-looking, user-friendly website or don't have one at all. An ugly, out-of-date website is worse than no website at all. If you're going to be on social media, dive in with both feet. Be active, alive, engaging, and present.

Remember you are engaging in a relationship with those that like or follow you, and you need to commit to them.

We are digital missionaries and if you invest in these critical areas, I'm sure you'll see much fruit. Obviously, this doesn't replace word-of-mouth and face-to-face connections, but it's a piece of a multi-faceted puzzle and one of many ways to make a lasting and good first impression.

MORE HELP:

There's a FREE church site self-assessment tool that creates an online consultation report to help you to look critically at your church website, and develop strategies to make it communicate to outsiders living in your area. Their questionnaire only takes three minutes to complete, then you can view your free 15-page consultation report about your church website, with specific recommendations on usability and strategy. The report also includes suggested further reading, and a highly-recommended video training seminar about church sites. Go

here to participate:
http://www.internetevangelismday.com/
church-site-design.php

For more help with your church's online
presence and all areas related to this book, go
here to sign-up for my free newsletter:
http://gregatkinson.com/subscribe-to-newsletter/

If you'd like me to evaluate your church's online
presence and send you a report (for a small fee),
email me at greg@gregatkinson.com.

TIP: Most church websites could be built and
managed in Wordpress (even if you have a
pro set it up). This is an easy way to edit and
manage a website with volunteers or staff.
Check out ChurchThemes.com. You'll thank
me.

BONUS: Use tools like Buffer.com or Hootsuite.
com to manage your social media accounts. It
will simplify things and save you lots of time.

2
PARKING

After I have evaluated a church's online presence from a distance, I then fly or drive to the church and make an onsite visit. The first thing I do when I arrive on Saturday is drive to the church and look at the parking lot appeal. This includes everything from the parking lot itself, to the grounds, the outside of the building, the road signage, and the overall feel of the campus. Is it welcoming to outsiders or guests? Let's explore each and then discuss what I look for on a Sunday.

First, when I arrive on a Saturday, it means I'm putting directions into my GPS that I got from somewhere. Was it the church's website? Was it on my mobile phone? Was it from the church's Facebook page? Or all of the above? I want to stress again how crucial it is for your church's service times and directions to be highly visible. Another way to put it is "easy to see or spot." I shouldn't have to look around and click a link to find out where and when you meet.

The first thing I notice once I arrive on campus is the church's sign by the road. Believe it or not, this says a ton about a church. Your road signage will speak to how much you care about guests. When cars drive by your church each day do they see a welcoming sight or an ugly deterrent?

Let's dig deeper. Buckle up! If your church's road sign has a marquee, this can be a good thing or this can be a terrible thing. There is nothing worse than cheesy sayings on a church sign. Number one, they are offensive. Does anyone think "Turn or burn" is going to save a soul? Seriously?

When my last church moved locations, we renovated a building that had a road sign with a marquee. I remember one influential person in the church emailed me about ways to use the sign to reach people. This person meant well, but her suggestions were cheesy and offensive all at once. I simply emailed her back and said, "No thanks. We're going to go in a different direction with how we use the sign."

We decided to use the sign to publicize upcoming events, and most often to list the title of each week's sermon. If you have a good sense of humor (which is vital in life, ministry, and leadership), I encourage you to follow Ed Stetzer's blog (edstetzer.com) and see his weekly "Church Signs of the Week" posts. They are hilarious and scary at the same time. It's scary, sad, and frustrating to think of what some church's put on their sign. Think, folks, think!

I recently consulted with a church in San Antonio, Texas and they had this same issue. They had a road sign with a marquee, which they used to put the name of the sermon series and message title up on. The problem? The pastor came up with the series and sermon titles and they were too churchy, too deep, and too wordy. He was doing a series entitled "Omega Logos." It's a good title for a seminary class or lecture but not an inviting title that makes people want to come to your church. I explained this to them, and they received it well.

Notice I'm not talking about content, delivery, topical vs expository, traditional vs contemporary, etc. As I've often said, "God uses all kinds of churches to reach all kinds of people." What I am talking about is packaging and presentation. Your series and message titles must be intriguing, interesting, and understandable to someone who knows nothing about

God or the Bible. It simply comes down to being effective. When a lost person in a car drives by at 35 miles per hour and glances at your road sign, are they going to think, "Hmm. Sounds interesting." Or are they going to think, "What the heck does that mean?"

Obviously, another aspect of every church's sign (whether it has a marquee or not) is that it looks sharp (well-designed with an attractive logo) and works at night. I was working with another church in Texas that had a great-looking sign during the day, but when I drove by their church at night, some of the sign's lights were burned out and not working. Whoever is in charge of maintenance at your church needs to be on top of this and keep an eye on your sign and other lights on the exterior of your church building.

Concerning the parking lot and the grounds, they should be well kept. This should be obvious. What sort of message does it send to your congregation or guests if your campus looks like a junkyard? Invite someone that doesn't go to your church and has "new eyes" like a secret shopper to walk around your property. Ask them what needs trimming, cutting, fixing, repairing, painting, cleaning, etc. I do this everywhere I go. One church I worked with had a huge pile of concrete parking barriers piled up in their back parking lot. Who wants to see that? Get some guys to haul it off.

Churches that can afford it and see it as a priority take good care of their parking lot. They get it sealed and painted on a regular schedule. They make sure that everyone can see the lines of the parking lot and know where to park their car.

Take note of this information from the Americans with Disabilities Act (ADA) website: "How many accessible parking spaces are needed? One of every six accessible parking spaces, or fraction thereof, must be 'van-accessible'. For example: A parking lot with 400 total spaces needs eight accessible spaces, and two of those eight spaces must be van-accessible. Accessible spaces must connect to the shortest possible accessible route to the accessible building entrance or facility they serve."[11]

As far as signage, the ADA website states: "Accessible parking spaces must be identified by signs that include the International Symbol of Accessibility. Signs at van-accessible spaces must include the additional phrase 'van-accessible'. Signs should be mounted so that the lower edge of the sign is at least five (5) feet above the ground. This helps ensure visibility both for motorists and local enforcement officials."[12]

I'll cover more about signage in a future chapter, but obviously you need to have designated handicapped parking spots and signs. I'm also a big fan of guest parking signs. I recommend that every church have designated parking for guests. I also share Tim Steven's "Three Growth Lids" with each church that I consult with.[13] I agree with Tim. We must remove as many barriers as we possibly can. That's what this whole book is about. We should make it easy for guests to find your church, arrive and park, and then find their way into the building.

Three Growth Lids from Tim Stevens:

- Parking - This is why Visitor Parking is so crucial. If it's difficult for newcomers to go to your church, they won't go.
- Children - If it looks like a child is entering a room that is too small, understaffed, or unsafe, then the parents will not return.
- Seats - Your growth will begin to level off when your space is 80 percent full.

* Every growing church should have
someone who is constantly watching these
three lids and looking into the future.

Another thing I'm a big fan of is parking lot attendants or a church with a parking lot team. I'm actually upset if I go to a church and no one is in the parking lot greeting me with a wave and showing me to my parking space. Why do I get upset? Because it says so much. If you are expecting guests and you want to make their first visit as smooth as possible (remember we're removing barriers), then why wouldn't you position servants in your parking lot to greet people and help them orientate. Especially if your church is busy and parking is at a premium!

Some churches have a large campus with multiple parking lots, and many have to walk a long way. I've seen amazing churches that run a parking shuttle (a golf cart) to drive people from the far away parking spots to the entrance of the church. This is a nice gesture and goes a long way towards making a good first impression. Obviously, if your church is small and has one parking lot, you don't need a shuttle. It's just a nice idea to lock away in your brain. It's the thought that counts. Let's seek to kill them with kindness.

Remember you've got ten minutes before a first impression settles into someone's mind. From the moment they drive onto your lot, until they enter your building, everything they see, hear, smell, and experience matters. It's hard to put into words. When I drive to or by certain churches, I get an impression (good or bad) by what I see on the outside. Some churches give off a funeral home vibe. Some churches seem vibrant or exciting. Some seem inviting and welcoming. There's a reason new churches don't have graveyards next to the church anymore. It gives an impression—a negative one.

So I encourage you to invite a guest to your church. Tell them you'll buy them lunch or coffee. Ask them for their impressions. Ask them what they think of your road sign, your parking lot, your grounds, and the outside of your building. Put careful thought into their feedback and give it serious consideration.

In a church where I served as campus pastor, I changed the name of our campus and got a new outdoor sign just based on the feedback of a newcomer who was confused by our name and branding. Always be teachable. Always be approachable. Always be open to constructive criticism. And when the time comes to act... execute. Be a change agent.

3
FIRST IMPRESSIONS

First impressions matter—big time! Sometimes there's no coming back from a bad experience. In this chapter we're going to look at several things that encompass a guest's first impression of your church, from your First Impressions Team, Guest Services Team, or Hospitality Team, to your Parking Lot Team, to your ushers, greeters, your welcome desk or information center, and third place environments like cafés and bookstores.

Be wise when you engage with those
outside the faith community; make
the most of every moment and every
encounter. – Colossians 4:5 (VOICE)

Your First Impressions Team, Guest Services, or Hospitality Team can be used by God to make people feel at ease when they arrive. Remember, it's all about removing barriers. Mark Waltz writes: "The late Stephen Covey's second habit of highly effective people is 'Begin with the end in mind.' Before our guests arrive, we need to envision the experience we desire for them. If we can see that experience clearly, we can create a road map to lead them there."[14]

What do you want people to feel? What emotions do you want them to experience within the first few minutes? What do you want them to see, touch, hear, and smell? It may help to put yourself in their shoes and ask what they want to feel. What do any of us want to feel in a new place? I don't know about you, but when I go somewhere new, I want to feel special and valued.

In far too many churches, leaders and pastors put their leftovers on their First Impressions Team. And these people can sense it. They realize they can't sing, play drums, run lights, teach a small group, or some other esteemed position, so when they get placed on the First Impressions Team, they feel they are doing the least important ministry in the church. Nothing could be further from the truth!

When I work with churches, I exhort them to put their best and brightest, their positive, smiling, warmest personalities on their front lines. Starting with the Parking Lot Team and moving inside to your First Impressions Team (greeters, ushers and those working the Welcome Desk or Information Center). These people need to be friendly and welcoming. Most of all, they need to know how vital their role is to the mission of the church.

How do you cast this vision? Repetition. You hold regular team meetings and you huddle up first thing Sunday morning before people start to arrive. At my church, our first service started at 9:30 am, so we would meet with and pray with our First Impressions Team each week at 9:00 am.

We use that time each week to cast vision, tell them how important what they are doing is, and most importantly (say this every week), remind them that *today is someone's first time visiting your church*. Every week you have guests, and you can't lose sight of this. It's why I'm writing this book.

In *First Impressions*, Mark Waltz reminds us: "Rather than presenting a 99-page how-to manual, paint a broad-stroke picture of the atmosphere you want to create." He goes on to write, "If your teams get too caught up in completing their ministry assignments correctly without first engaging their hearts in the mission, your environment will be characterized by performers of tasks. The atmosphere may be efficient, but it will likely be chilly as well. Cast vision; teach the mission of your church and ministry; describe clear objectives. Then invite your teams to help create an environment in which these objectives can be met."[15]

Yes. Yes. Amen! Mark's book covers how to train your teams in detail and is a resource I refer to often. I highly encourage you to buy a copy of his book for you, your leadership, and your team. It's a great read. So who should you look for on your First Impressions Team, Guest Services, or Hospitality Team? Personally, I look for people with a great personality, a good smile, and no socially awkward things going on, and then I make "the ask." I ask them to be a key part of our First Impressions Team. Remember you have ten minutes before a first impression sets in. The person a guest sees and interacts with in those ten minutes means more than your music for the day, or even the pastor's sermon. Pastors, pay attention. Your First Impressions team has just as much an impact on guests—if not more—than your sermons.

While we're discussing your teams, I've got a bone to pick. This comes from years of my own ministry experience and years as a consultant. I want to talk about your Parking Lot Team, ushers and greeters, and my pet peeves. First, the Parking Lot Team: Nothing drives me crazier than seeing parking lot attendants standing next to each other. There should never be two people (or more) standing next to each other and talking. Parking lot attendants should be spread out across your parking lot communicating with hand signals and/or walkie-talkies.

When I see parking lot attendants bunched up and talking to one another it tells me they don't know their purpose. They don't realize that their focus and attention needs to be on greeting and pointing people in the right direction. Nothing is worse than driving by two parking lot attendants deep in conversation that don't even acknowledge you. Trust me, I've experienced it and it's a horrible first impression of your church. Give your parking lot attendants posts or positions and have them stay spread out. Remind them to focus on their responsibility and to smile and wave at cars as they drive pass. Remember the atmosphere we want to create.

Moving on to greeters. Have you ever experienced over-zealous greeters? Greeters that freak you out because they're too happy, too nosy, or too obnoxious? Greeters need to spread out too, and leave space for people to walk. Please don't form a wall that makes it awkward for people when entering your building. I had a bad experience at a large and well-known church one time. I can't tell you how many hands I had to shake to enter their building. I think you get the point.

Finally, one last bone to pick, and that's with ushers. I think we over-simplify when it comes to training ushers. I can't tell you how many churches I've visited or consulted with who had told their ushers "Stand here and give each person a bulletin as they pass." This is a poor vision indeed. If your only job is to hand someone a bulletin, you don't take it seriously. You don't do anything else outside that and it's easy to get in conversation with other ushers. If you haven't picked up on it, I don't like for conversations to be going on with team members. I think it's rude and a horrible first impression. No one wants to feel like they're interrupting your discussion to get a bulletin or find a seat.

Speaking of finding a seat, that *is* the job of the usher. I've seen churches that put bulletins on a small table and let the ushers usher. I love this! Ushers should be seating people and helping those with special needs, wheelchairs, etc.

I recently consulted with First Baptist Dallas, Texas. Their ushers were amazing. They were effective and efficient and they worked as a team to find seats for everyone in a crowded auditorium. It was a joy to see. 12Stone Church in Atlanta has a wonderful usher manual. It reads: "Take initiative! This is huge. The cardinal sin of an usher is to not pay attention. At all times watch what is going on in your section and jump in to handle it. The only wrong choice is to do nothing. Never assume 'someone' else is taking care of the need. Pay attention, take initiative, make it happen!"[16]

In numerous churches, ushers also collect the offering. Let's encourage ushers to smile during this time of the worship service. God loves a cheerful giver, and God loves a cheerful usher. In many churches, ushers also serve communion. This is something that requires training and a certain level of excellence, as does collecting the offering. Please don't rush people when they're taking communion. That is a special and reverent time, and people need to be able to worship as they partake. In many churches, ushers count attendance. I've seen this done well, and I've seen this be a distraction. No one wants to see someone walk to the front of the auditorium and point at people as they mouth the count. Please ask your ushers to count from a distance or a high-vantage point and try their best not to disturb congregants that are trying to focus on the sermon.

I have one last bone to pick with all team members, and this is a big one! I had to battle this at my last church and suppose it will always be an issue in today's digital world. My last bone to pick is to make sure your servant leaders are hands-free. Meaning they shouldn't be holding a cup of coffee or their cell phone.

Imagine a single mom struggling to corral her toddlers and holding an infant's carrier in one hand, walking in from the parking lot, and the guy or gal at the door is too distracted by their phone to open the door for her. Or he's trying to open the door and not spill his coffee on her and her children. This is where vision-casting comes in, friends. You must talk to your team about sacrifice. The reason they arrive early (at least 30 minutes before a service) is to talk to friends, get some coffee and do other stuff that they shouldn't be doing while they're serving. Once it's go-time, they must be hands-free and focused. Okay, I'm stepping down off my soapbox. Moving on.

Most churches have some kind of welcome center or information center. This desk should be staffed by someone friendly, caring, and well-trained. They need to know where everything that a guest may want to get to is located. They need to be ready to assist, answer questions, and give them a welcome gift or packet (if your church does that).

I also recommend that you have at least two people operate the desk. You never know when one is going to need to leave to help someone. For example, if you have a large campus or confusing building layout, and a mom with three children comes up to the desk and asks where she takes her children, you should say, "I'll be glad to show you!" and then escort her to the children's check-in desk or station. When that person leaves to escort the mom, the desk is continuing to be operated by the person or people remaining behind.

Next, let's talk about third place environments. These are special designated areas for conversation, spaces like coffee shops, cafes, or bookstores. Not every church has these areas, whether it's due to space limitation or not a part of their ministry philosophy. I do think if you're going to do it, you should do it with excellence.

I once consulted with a church of 12,000 people that had the ugliest café and café sign I've ever seen. It looked like a third grader drew a sign on a piece of paper and then taped it to a post. Really? If you're going to have a café or coffee shop, do it well and serve people well. Think of your experience at Starbucks or your local coffee shop. Remember Chick-fil-A and how well they serve people.

It takes patient and kind people to serve in these roles. However, some of the best baristas I've ever experienced at churches or even Starbucks were teenagers. Don't be afraid to have young people serve in your First Impressions Ministry. That goes for this whole chapter and book. Teenagers can serve in the parking lot, can be greeters, can be ushers, and can serve coffee.

In May of 2014 Michael Trent, Founder and Idea Engineer at Third Place Consulting, wrote a guest blog post on my blog: GregAtkinson.com. He talked about how people that serve in third place environments should approach their job. Here's what he wrote:

> "When leading (which is serving) from behind the bar, consider your:
>
> **Positioning:** of your *heart*, knowing why you are there; of

your *head*, having an awareness of your surroundings before people enter; and of your *body* to best be able to access your serving tools and the people you serve.

Peripheral vision: Your positioning in an environment should be one that allows you to have a good view of who and what is going on around you. We've all been to a place where it felt like the person serving us forgot we were even there. Peripheral vision will provide a big picture and a context.

Posture: Your body language can often speak louder than your words. No matter what statistic you read, the truth is, the majority of how we communicate is through our non-verbals (and that does not include technology...please don't miss that). How you sit, lean, stand, or walk can say a lot more than you might think; so keep that in mind and I promise people won't mind.

Perspective: Keeping open ears and an open heart, you'll find moments of seriousness, of laughter, of sympathy, even of empathy; moments both heavy and light where you can find some of the greatest and most authentic connections. My suggestion, especially when you quickly pick up a negative vibe…is to always side with keeping the 'glass half full' (or even higher in each conversation).

Pronunciation: Next time you hear someone lacking pronunciation, see if there doesn't also seem to be a disconnection to the present. Maybe that sounds like a strange leadership lesson? As we find ourselves mentally and physical communicating through so many 'shortcut' version of communication, it is sad and surprising how something this simple is being effected. One of the best ways to focus on pronunciation is to focus on the person you're talking to, be there, not somewhere else.

Perception: So much here could be said, let's just say it's about my concern for the lost art of listening. Take time to listen to what people are sharing; and always remember, that everyone has a history, a story, and a future.

and Pour Carefully: No matter if you are a cafe pastor, lead pastor, leader in your business, leader in your home, you get the point…our lives are constantly being poured out into the lives of others, let us take that to heart, consider it with our minds, and pour carefully through our actions."[17]

Good advice and principles to serve and lead by. In all the roles I've written about in this book, it's important to be focused, tuned in, and listening.

Now we move to an important subject: Coffee. I want to go on the record that I think it's good for churches to serve coffee. You don't have to have a coffee shop and sell drinks. You can set up some coffee dispensers and offer free regular and decaf coffee with sugar, sweeteners, and creamer. I'll talk about this more in the chapter on smell, but coffee is one of the best smells in the world (whether you like to drink it or not). It's a great first impression and the offer of free coffee says a lot about your church and the experience you want your guests to have. It's a sign of hospitality and it's where life happens these days.

Mark Batterson writes that coffee shops are modern-day wells. In his article "Postmodern Wells: Creating a Third Place," he discusses why his church built and owns a coffee shop called Ebenezers:

"So why would we build a coffeehouse instead of a church building? Especially when nobody on our staff had any coffeehouse experience or expertise before we started construction. The motivation is simple. Jesus didn't hang out at synagogues. Jesus hung out at wells. Wells were more than just a place to draw water. Wells were *natural gathering places* in ancient culture. Think of them as third places.

Jesus didn't expect people to come to him. He crossed ancient cultural boundaries and went to them. And that is what the incarnation is all about. So instead of building a traditional church building where people gather once a week, we built a postmodern well where people gather all day every day. And instead of water, we serve coffee"[18]

When I want to get to know someone new, I say, "Can I buy you a cup of coffee?" I can't tell you how many meetings I do at coffee shops. They are modern-day wells and the place where conversations happen. If you want to make someone feel welcomed and at ease when they walk in your building, put coffee out. Trust me, it goes a long way toward making a good first impression.

And yes, this means this is something you will need to *invest in* and include in your budget. There are lots of ways to accomplish this, whether it be a weekly expense in your budget, or whether you have people provide it each week or donate money to cover expenses.

At my last church, we gave out coffee and donuts, and we couldn't afford to pay for donuts anymore, so I found someone in the church to pay for the donuts. They didn't want to see the donuts go away and offered to cover the costs. Most churches can't do donuts or snacks. That's fine. Coffee is a great first impression. Pray about this matter and seek God's leading for everything we've discussed so far.

4
THE SENSE OF SMELL

When I first walk into the building of a church I'm visiting or secret shopping, the first thing I do is smell. Your guests do this too, though unconsciously. Concerning smell, let me share with you a passage from a previous book I wrote:

> "It's important that no church ever underestimates the sense of smell. While sight is the strongest sense for short-term memory, the sense of smell is the strongest and most vivid for long-term memories. If you've ever smelled something and had memories you hadn't thought of in years come flooding back, that's your sense of smell in action. Every church has the potential for positive or negative smells. Mold is a bad smell. Coffee is a good smell.

Bleach is a bad smell. Citrus is a good smell. Many churches have restrooms that are disgusting and smell like urine. This lack of attention to detail can be costly and discourage many from ever returning. As best you can, try to walk into the lobby or entrance of your church with a new nose."[19]

This one chapter and principle is so simple, so easy, so seemingly insignificant, that you may be tempted to skip over it. Please don't. Let me try to impart to you how powerful the sense of smell is. I'll share a few examples from my own life. I have met a woman before or hugged someone at church and smelled a perfume that I recognized as the same perfume my girlfriend in high school wore. The smell over twenty years later immediately transported me back in time. I met a woman before and immediately recognized her perfume as my third grade teacher's perfume. I was immediately transported back thirty years in time. I've walked into churches that smelled like funeral homes. It brings you down. I've walked into churches that smelled like hospitals or had a pungent bleach smell. I wanted to quickly leave.

If you don't believe how powerful and persuasive the sense of smell is, I'd encourage you to do some research and see how many stores have invested millions of dollars researching which smells encourage you to shop longer, buy more, become hungry, etc.

Have you ever walked into a department store and seen machines in the corners of the store pumping out a mist of aroma into the air? I have. They're present in most shopping malls. They are also present in large churches, like Elevation Church in Charlotte, NC.

I was once contacted by a company that sold units that put pleasing smells out into the air and was working with large churches like Elevation, as well as department stores and hotels. Here is some of the email exchange from a representative of ScentAir:

"Hi Greg,

I hope you are doing well! I wanted to reach out to you as we do a tremendous amount of work in this industry across the country and I am fairly 'new' with this industry and wanted to pick your brain a little perhaps next week. We provide means for businesses to enhance their 'customer experience' with scent marketing and branding. We have some very unique marketing strategies that are very powerful and memorable and that is the key point.

We are best known for our branding with Hotels, Casinos, Resorts, Retail stores, and Disney World; however, it is obvious this is a great opportunity as well to enhance such an emotional experience already. We currently work with dozens of large churches like Elevation in Charlotte that have given fantastic feedback. Such as 'relaxing, feels welcoming, and in counseling areas helps reduce stress' as well as a brand message…

Creating a nurturing and calming atmosphere is important in the church. Scent can help you create this environment and experience for your guests. Church services nationwide count on ScentAir to help transform their environments. Have you considered the role of scent in your business? ScentAir wants to help make a difference with your guests…"

Did You Know: 75% of the emotions
we generate are from what we smell.
Your family experience matters!

I know what some of you are thinking: We're not a department store. We're not a hotel. We're not a business! Trust me. I get it. But if it has been scientifically proven that the sense of smell has a huge impact on the way we feel and process emotions, then I think it is wise to take it seriously. You may not need to buy from a company like ScentAir, but what you do need to do is walk into your church with a new nose (or have a guest do it) and see what you smell.

Our sense of smell profoundly plays into what we perceive (first impression) and how we make judgments on the experience (will we return?). I know you may not put a lot of stock into something companies do to get customers to buy more, but I hope you'll trust my experience and knowledge of the matter. I can't tell you how many church restrooms I walked into that stunk of urine. It was unbearable. I wanted to run out of there. The churches that I've visited that smelled like bleach or a funeral home, or a hospital, many guests will never return to them. This is why it's so important to offer coffee and get that pleasing aroma in the air. Again, this chapter is simple and seems insignificant, but how you respond to it, determines how you keep and retain guests. I pray you'll take this seriously.

5
SIGNAGE

Let me point out something we often forget. People that visit our churches for the first time are often nervous, stressed, tense, uneasy, and looking for an excuse to turn around and walk back out. This is why first impressions are so vital to a church's growth. We should do everything we can to remove barriers and distractions, including potentially stressful and frustrating situations like not knowing where to take your children, how to find the restroom, or even where to find the auditorium. I've worked with churches so large that the first time I was there, I had no idea where the auditorium was, and I walked in a totally different building that was not the auditorium.

This brings me to a crucial point: **Never assume people know anything.** Map out your guest experience step-by-step. Take nothing for granted. Geoff Surratt, in his book *The*

Effective Church, writes, "Churches are notoriously bad with signage; signs are often difficult to read, confusing and scarce."[20] I agree and I think we need to do a better job as a whole.

"By opening up to others, you'll
prompt people to open up with
God..." – Matthew 5:16 (MSG)

I've visited numerous churches over the years (both as a guest and as a consultant), and I can vouch that signage is a serious issue. I've gotten lost more times than I like to think about. So let's look at the who, what, when, where, and how.

WHO

Get your Communications Team on this if you have one. If not, go to a knowledgeable layperson, consultant, local pastor in your city, outside company, or anyone trustworthy that can give you a new set of eyes. Whoever creates and designs your signage should be a professional designer with a good eye for sharp and modern design. Typography is huge and should not be overlooked. Talk with your designer about what vibe and style you want your church to reflect and then keep it consistent throughout.

WHAT

Walk your church's property and look for all exterior and then interior signage, or the lack thereof. You need to designate signage for guest parking, entrances, service times, a special children's entrance (if you have one), restrooms (this is huge), and your auditorium. Remember, never assume people know where anything is.

All of your signage needs to be tied into your church's overall branding and look like it belongs. I hope that makes sense. Don't have part of your signs one material (like plastic or vinyl) and then some of your signs in wood. Make sure they all match the same feel and vibe, even if the colors are different for different areas of your building (such as children's and youth ministry, café, etc.).

WHEN

If you haven't sufficiently covered your campus with appropriate signage, I suggest you tackle this immediately. You never get a second chance to make a first impression. Make this a priority right now for your organization.

WHERE

Walk your church's property (with someone new) and see if they know how to get around. Make note of signs that should be there and fix ones that are missing. Also, make sure you place the signs at the right height. Once a crowd of people are walking through a lobby or children's hallway, signs get covered up unless they are overhead.

The reason it is key to have someone visit your campus (whether a local volunteer, someone from out of town, or a secret shopper) is because they will speak openly and honestly about how easy it is to navigate your church's campus and layout. Once I worked with a church that had two buildings. When I pulled into the front parking lot, there was a sign on one building that read "AUDITORIUM" and a sign on the other building that read "CHILDREN." The problem was that they had a back parking lot and if you parked back there, there were no signs telling you which building was which. Again, never assume people know where to go.

HOW

Steve Fogg wrote a guest blog post for Church Marketing Sucks on interior signage. One of his points was to walk through your facility. He explains, "Explore your facility as though you are a first time visitor. Find out where the visitors will need to make critical decisions about where they need to go. Write out your navigation ideas. Invite a friend who isn't familiar with your facility to walk around with you and see if it makes sense to them. It's tempting to skip this step, but you can probably walk your facility blindfolded. Get that outside perspective."[21] This is why I love doing what I do as a secret shopper. I can't tell you how many times I've gotten lost at a church without proper signage.

Another great point Steve brought up is to talk to your

stakeholders. He writes, "People use your church facility for all kinds of reasons. Get agreement on names of rooms and your central point of connection. For example, our weekend welcome desk in our church foyer is also our church office reception. Suppliers instinctively go to reception but we called it 'welcome desk' for simplicity's sake. Different visitors are looking for different destinations and you have to make a decision on who has priority."[22]

On writing about creating interior signage at his church in Melbourne, Australia, Steve wrote it's "not as fun, but vital. Successfully delivering a signage system isn't as cool as developing a website or creating video for others, but it can be a vital part of your visitor experience and make their first visit that much easier."[23] I couldn't agree more. It's a huge part of your guests' experience.

We've covered the Who, What, When, Where and How, but we really need to talk about the Why. I was recently consulting with a Baptist Association. I had built them a website and was training them on social media. The Director of Missions had a suggestion which I knew was a bad idea and I said, "No, we don't want to do that." I hung up the phone and went about my business. Then it occurred to me that I hadn't given him the "Why," so I called him back and said, "Let me tell you why that is a bad idea and why I don't want to do it. Once he understood the why, it made sense and he got on board with my line of thinking.

So here's the *Why*: Because we care and want guests to have a wonderful and meaningful experience. Friends, if guests are so rattled and unnerved from trying to find the restroom, and the children's check-in and then the auditorium, they will be so flustered and frustrated and maybe mad, that they will not only zone out during the music and message, but they will miss out on what God may be wanting to do in their life.

Guest Services and First Impressions, which include signage, are the first line of defense. We remove barriers and distractions, so that our guests can focus on what God wants to do in their heart. I have a friend that reminds me that people need to know they matter to us before they hear they matter to God. This is the *Why*. So, if we know we've got to make it easy for our guests to navigate our property and building, the question becomes "Can you give me some help?" Absolutely. This is the heart behind this book. Concerning signage, Geoff Surratt gives some great tips for better signage:[24]

Signs are for first-time guests

After attending your church two or three times people know where everything is. Look at your signs look through the eyes of someone who has never been on your campus, never spoken to anyone at your church and never been in a church like yours before. Imagine how you' feel walking into a mosque for the first time. What signs would help you the most?

Signs must answer four basic questions men ask

Men do not want to go your Information Desk, Welcome Center or Hospitality Booth; they want to figure it out for themselves. Your signs are there to help them. Here are the four questions men walking into your church for the first time want answere:

- *Where am I supposed to go?*
- *Where are my kids supposed to go?*
- *Where is the bathroom?*
- *Is there coffee?*

Your missions wall, ministry booths an kiosks full of flyers o not answer these four questions, big, obvious signs should.

Signs must be easy to use

Signs at eye level or below become invisible (and worthless) when there is a crowd. Signs that are too high are also of little value.

Signs must be easy to read

Another church has a children's ministry sign in the main lobby (which is big enough to lan. a 747 in) that is 15 feet off the groun., three miles from the front door and in a 14-point font. You could attend the church for months before realizing the sign is even there. I can't imagine a first time guest ever fin.ing it.

The goal of sign placement, design and font size is readability. All of the signs at a large church in Seattle are huge black and white banners with one or two words. (RESTROOMS, ADULT AUDI-TORIUM, CHILDREN'S AUDITORIUM). That's probably overkill unless your signs are for first time guests who .on't want to ask directions. Which they are.

Signs must never use insider lingo

This is where churches make the biggest mistake. They come up with cool, cute or trendy names for things that obscure what the *thing actually is. I'm extremely guilty of this using names like Treasure Cove, Harbor Town and Nitro instead of Babies, Elementary, and Jr High.*

It's fine to have fun names, just ∂on't make them the main thing on directional signs. (Adding age categories in a tiny font at the bottom doesn't help).

Beyond the catchy names are the churchy labels, what exactly is a Worship Center or a Sanctuary? We might as well go back to the names Narthex and Crypt. Everyone knows what an auditorium is and everyone knows that is where they're probably supposed to go. Call it what it is so first time guests can fin∂ it.

I must admit, I struggled for a season with making up insider names for ministries. After consulting for years and getting lost numerous times, I came to the conclusion that Geoff is right. So when we designed the interior signage for our new campus at my last church, we went with generic names over the doorways. For example, the student ministry doorway had *Students* over the top of it, even though their ministry was called Unite. Would a guest know what Unite is? No. Again, never assume a guest knows anything and do all you can to enhance and smooth over their experience at your church.

6

CHILDREN'S MINISTRY

But Jesus said, "Let the children come to
me. Don't stop them! For the Kingdom
of Heaven belongs to those who are like
these children." – Matthew 19:14 (NLT)

Children's ministry is part of the "Big 3" that I look for when
I do a secret shopper visit. My Big 3 are First Impressions,
Children's Ministry, and Security. I look at everything that I
cover in this book when I do a consultation, but these are the
three main ones. Children's ministry is key to attracting and
keeping families.

I'm proud to be a part of a multigenerational church that con-
siders every age when we meet. At my church, the children

participate with the Orange curriculum, which I highly recommend. When I visit churches, the three things that I must see and look for are: Is your children's ministry clean, safe, and secure? Let's look at each of the three things every children's ministry must be in more detail.

CLEAN

Germs—every church has them. However, if my kids consistently come home sick from church, I'm going to catch on and not return. One of the best practices I've seen many churches do is to place hand sanitizer dispensers throughout the building and in every classroom. This is wonderful.

Being clean is also being aware of and sensitive to the seasons. If it's flu season, be aware and be safe. Don't check a child into the classroom if they're running a fever and/or sick. It's your responsibility to protect the masses, even if that means upsetting one family who wants to drop off a sick child.

In October of 2014, my family visited Fellowship Dallas in Dallas, Texas. This was during the time that the Ebola outbreak was fresh, and the first patient at a Dallas hospital had died. When my wife went to drop off our kids in the children's ministry that weekend, they checked each child's temperature. They didn't take any chances and this made us feel safe and loved.

Also, when I say, "clean," I don't just mean germ-free. I mean neat and well-kept rooms. If a room is messy, dirty, and cluttered, it gives a bad impression to the parent and makes them want to take their children out of the room. You don't want parents distracted in the worship service thinking about what they saw when they dropped their children off.

SAFE

Every room where children learn and play must be safe. This is a simple concept. You can't have any jagged edges, rough corners, or sharp objects that can poke out a child's eye. If your room is not safe, I'm not leaving my kid. For parents that do leave their child, they may not be able to concentrate and worship during the service because they fear for their child's safety.

Even worse, God forbid something happens and a child gets hurt. If your room was not safe and the accident could have been prevented, you and your church will be liable and could get a bad reputation. One single accident or accusation could lead to news coverage and bad PR for the church. Much worse, a child could be hurt or damaged for the rest of their life. Children are precious and should be protected at all costs.

Safety also includes those who work with your children. Every child worker must go through a background check. No exceptions. I was recently talking with a pastor that said none of their children's ministry volunteers had been through a background check. I was disturbed and shocked. He knew he needed to change that, but I don't think he's moving fast enough.

Safety also includes that you are staffed properly and adequately. If I'm dropping my baby off into a nursery with one volunteer and ten babies, I'm turning around and leaving. Make sure you have a good ratio of children to volunteers. Safety also includes the view into the room. Many children's rooms have big windows that parents can look into. Also, most churches have windows in their doors, a half-door, or a Dutch door that allows people to see in, but keeps the children in the classroom. You don't want children wandering down the hall.

Lastly, always escort children to the bathroom (same gender). I can't tell you how many times as a secret shopper, that I've been able to stand and wait in a child bathroom at a church that didn't have proper security. We must protect our children and do whatever it takes to see that they grow up without shame and hurt.

SECURE

When I say, "secure," I'm mainly focusing on the children's check-in and checkout procedures, with a laser focus on their checkout procedure. You need to do whatever it takes to make sure that whoever is supposed to pick up children is the one that actually picks them up. I was talking with a pastor the other day that had a divorced dad pick up his children without the mom knowing it. There was a lot of drama and it could have been avoided.

Security also means every entrance and exit of the children's area and facilities are covered with volunteers that only let parents in and out. I was just at a great church in California last week that had every single entry and exit covered, and it was a beautiful thing to see.

Tim Stevens has written about his theory on three growth lids. One of the growth lids that he says every church ought to keep an eye on is children's ministry. Tim writes, "If it looks like a child is entering a room that is too small, understaffed, or unsafe, then the parents will not return."[25]

As a secret shopper, when I check out a church's children's ministry, I ask several questions about security. How easy is it to get to the nursery, classrooms, or child bathrooms? Do you have to present a matching sticker (from the church's database system and/or children's check-in software) when you pick up your child from their class?

Is there a proper ratio of children's workers to children? Do the children get escorted out of the classroom and to the bathroom? What is the layout of your children's facility like? Do you have to get buzzed in for entrance? Do you have to be escorted down a hallway during a service? Is there a back exit or entrance where children can go outside? Is it secure and safe? Is it protected from someone that walked up to that exit from the parking lot?

All these questions must be thought through with great detail and clarity. When we designed the new children's wing at my last church, we put in security doors at the entrance to the children's wing that could only be opened with a key card (which only staff and security team members had).

Not only that, there was only one way in and out of the children's wing. If you got allowed in by a key card, you were escorted down the hallway and there was no back exit. The only way one could leave was to walk back out the same doors they entered at the check-in area. I was proud of our security and systems in place. We kept attenders' children and guests' children safe, and their minds were at ease.

Your church may not be laid out like that. You may have a less than ideal floor plan for your children's area. It's important that you step up your security team presence to make up for the lack of locks and key card entrances. I always encourage church leaders to train their people to ask one simple question when they see someone wandering through the children's hallway or going somewhere they shouldn't: "May I help you?" Read that again.

Don't miss this. This is the perfect question. If they truly are lost and innocent, this allows you to help them without coming across as rude, mean or accusatory. If they are up to no good, this simple question is a deterrent. I've seen people respond, "No thanks. I'll let myself out." It's important that your children's ministry worker or security team member make direct eye contact when they ask the question and be ready to escort them out. Whatever you do, don't take your eye off of them the entire time they are in close range to your children's ministry.

Obviously, I look at the children's facilities, decor, atmosphere, curriculum, and what my kids think after I pick them up. Creativity goes a long way in children's ministry, and you can never emphasize enough how important it is for children's ministries to be *fun*. I want my kids to learn about Jesus, but I also want them to have the time of their life and love going to church.

These three things I shared today (clean, safe, and secure) are just basic building blocks of a next-level children's ministry and are often overlooked by some churches. If you will focus on the entire experience for your kids, including these three keys, you'll have an irresistible children's ministry.

Whatever your children's curriculum, whether you study the sermon, create your own curriculum, or you do the Orange curriculum or another one, make sure your servant leaders are trained well, encouraged, loved on, and supported. Let them know that they are important to your church's mission and that they are not babysitting. They have a wonderful opportunity to teach young children about God. I am thankful for the Sunday School teachers that invested in me when I was young, teaching me the books of the Bible and classic stories about Noah, Abraham, Moses, David and Goliath, and many more.

Just like you put your people with great personalities on your First Impressions Team, you should find and train people that love children to work with children. They need to be the right fit for that type of ministry. Do you want to know if they love children and want to invest in the next generation? Simply ask them. And remember, never place anyone in the children's ministry area that didn't pass the background check (this includes security team members).

This goes without saying, but I don't want to assume anything. Children are your best secret shoppers for how effective your children's ministry actually is. Ask your kids and other children in the church how they like their class. Ask them what they're learning. Ask them if they feel safe and loved. Ask them if anything inappropriate has ever taken place. Children are brutally honest and will give you a good pulse on what's going on in your children's ministry.

Your children's ministry area doesn't have to look like Disney World or North Point, but it should look kid-friendly, safe, colorful (it just takes a gallon of paint), and like you value children and want them to enjoy church. I love stories of children that drag their parents to church. You never know how you will impact the next generation and their families through your children's ministry. Invest in keeping them safe. Invest in their leaders. Train them well and constantly cast the vision of your church to your servant leaders. They are a part of something special, and they need to be constantly refocused on that.

7
SECURITY

"But we prayed to our God and posted
a guard day and night to meet this
threat." – Nehemiah 4:9 (NIV)

The entire American church world woke up to the cruel
reality of the necessity of security on a Wednesday night in
September 1999. Larry Gene Ashbrook walked into Wedg-
wood Baptist Church in Texas and began shooting people.
Unspeakable horror and tragedy took place, and our lives as
Christians in the American church have never been the same
again.

One of the huge problems I see as I consult with churches
across the country is that most church leaders have never sat

down and intentionally and strategically thought through how and why they do security. I wish this wasn't important and that you didn't have to have some kind of security presence and procedures in place, but unfortunately, that's not the case. I'm sad to say that several churches have experienced the tragedy of shootings, not to mention molestation and kidnapping.

I'll never forget it. It was about five years ago and I was consulting with a well-known church of over 12,000 attendees. They have a gifted communicator as a pastor and a gifted worship leader, who is a recording artist. Their worship service experience is by all accounts amazing. I turned in my secret shopper report and did my review meeting with them via video conference. The executive pastor was ecstatic. He couldn't believe how truthful and brutally honest I was. What did I do?

I had a question at the end of the report that simply read, "Would I return to this church after my first visit?" My answer? "No." They were shocked. Their pastor led and spoke at conferences all over the world. He was an amazing preacher. Their worship leader was killer and someone that you hear on the radio. So, why would I not return for a second visit? It all came down to their security, or lack of. I didn't feel safe, and I didn't think my kids would be safe. They loved my honesty, made serious changes and are now a better church for it—a church where I would feel safe with my family.

Why is security such a big deal for me and others who may visit or attend your church? Here's the bottom-line: If I'm worried about my kids' safety, I'm not going to enjoy the worship service, and I will miss what God wants to do in my heart through the experience of corporate worship. And if uncomfortable, unsafe feelings continue, I will find somewhere else to worship. Your congregation and newcomers feel the same way.

I know what many of you are thinking because it's all too common. "We don't need security. We don't want to have it. It takes away from our warm, welcoming image. Is it really necessary?" Let me just say, "Yes. It is necessary."

I remember I was teaching a workshop at the National Outreach Convention in San Diego, and my topic was the subject of this book: What I look for when I do a secret shopper visit. I talked about security, and I could feel the tension in the room.

After the class, a pastor of a church of about 400 people came up to me and hugged me. He thanked me for validating what he felt. He said people thought he was crazy to have someone walk beside him and escort him as he walked around the church (even though they were only 400 people). I told him it was wise, and he was doing the right thing. He left encouraged. Regardless of your church's size, security measures have to be taken to ensure that your congregation, guests, and pastor are safe. It only takes *one* incident to do undoable damage and make you wish you had safety and security protocols in place. Let this book be your warning and don't wait for that incident to occur.

When I consulted with New Life Church in Colorado Springs, I was glad to see that the pastor had an escort near him at all times. He was available and accessible to the people (which is important and we'll discuss later), but he was safe and protected from anyone that may want to do him harm. I noticed the same thing when I consulted with Christ's Church of the Valley in Phoenix. Their pastor likes to walk around in-between services greeting people. I love this! But he had a security escort person walking with him everywhere he went. Friends, this is not overkill. This is smart.

I remember attending a church service at Old Fort Baptist Church in Summerville, South Carolina when I was in college. It was a normal day when all of a sudden a woman who was either having serious mental issues or was demon-possessed rushed the stage and started to scream at the pastor while he was in the middle of his sermon. She was guided off the stage by an usher and taken out in the lobby, screaming the whole way. I was eighteen years-old and that was when I became aware of church security.

A couple of years later, I was at a pastors' conference at First Baptist Jacksonville, where Jerry Vines was preaching. During a prayer, a man starting running down the aisle toward the pulpit. Thankfully, there were ushers and security personnel who didn't close their eyes during the prayer and tackled the man before he reached the stage. They escorted him out, and Jerry Vines continued to pray. These two stories were my introduction into church security necessity at an early age.

Church security encompasses a number of things. From your parking lot, to your children's ministry, to how your ushers operate, to an emergency medical response team, to financial security (like how you collect your tithes and offerings and how it's counted), to how you lock your building and leave it overnight. In the book *Serving by Safeguarding Your Church*, the author, Robert Welch, has a financial accountability security checklist. It's a thorough checklist with things like: "Do at least two ushers collect and take contributions to the counting space? Is there a secure counting room? Are at least two members of a counting team present at all times during a count? Are counting team members unrelated to each other?"[26] More great questions are listed in this checklist. I encourage you to get the book, read it, and give a copy to whoever oversees security at your church.

Robert Welch writes about the need to provide adequate lighting outside the building. He writes, "Law enforcement officials will tell you that the greatest deterrent to crime is providing a lighted area. By providing lighting to the building exterior, two objectives are met: (1) The lights will illuminate the area, making it safe for your parishioners and visitors to move around, and (2) the lights will deter the physical intrusion into the building of those who have no business entering."[27]

We recently installed lights on timers all around the building at my home church. It is a great deterrent and I love driving by and seeing it all lit up at night. Welch also reminds us to illuminate the parking lot. There's nothing worse than walking to your car at night in a dark parking lot. If your people, especially women, don't feel safe at your church, they won't come back. One should also make it a point to illuminate the entrances to the facility. This helps make people feel welcome, as well as provide security.

Security is the area that most churches fail when I do a secret shopper visit. They have prepped their First Impressions Team, they have good music, a good sermon, an impressive facility, and well-kept grounds and parking lot. But, too often, security takes a back seat to these items. Another thing that most churches are not prepared for are medical emergencies. That's why I ask every church if they have an Emergency Response Team (ERT). This team includes members who know to call 911 if someone has a heart attack or serious medical issue. These are team members that are wearing vibrating beepers during the service of their preference and are trained in CPR, defibrillator, and supplemental oxygen use.

Robert Welch writes, "Agree that the team's principal function will be to provide immediate intermediary care or action until municipal authorities respond. Develop a method of signaling the team into action. In my church we used the

Sunday school buzzer. Some churches give team members a local area pager, and I know of one church that uses a cell phone paging system."[28]

Think this isn't necessary? I've been in three services where people had heart attacks. In my first church where I served in college as a worship leader, a woman had a brain aneurism while I was leading the music and began screaming out in pain during the song. We had to call 911 and help her until the paramedics arrived. She was in tremendous pain and vomiting all over the place. All these memories and experiences were engrained in me at an early age

---

A prudent person foresees danger
and takes precautions. The simpleton
goes blindly on and suffers the
consequences. – Proverbs 22:3 (NLT)

Another thing that is simple, but not necessarily obvious, is to have first aid kits at various locations in your church (lobby, children's and youth ministry areas) and to make sure that your leaders know where to find them. I was proud two years ago when a child unfortunately cut his eye on a table while running around, but our leaders knew exactly where to find the first aid kit and how to take care of him.

Coach your ushers to be sensitive to security issues as well. As I mentioned in Chapter 3, ushers should be trained to do more than hand out bulletins. They should be ready to jump into action if an emergency like a heart attack happens, or if someone rushes the stage or pulpit and tries to attack the pastor. Just mentioning things like this regularly to your ushers will keep them sensitive and aware of issues if they were to occur.

It's important for your ushers to stay alert and take their role seriously. Usher responsibilities do not end once people are seated and the service starts. The usher should be ready for anything throughout the entire service. You never know when he or she might be needed. You should assign certain ushers to patrol the facility. One thing I love seeing when I visit churches is an usher acting as a hall monitor and keeping an eye out for anything suspicious or troublesome. It's especially good for them to monitor the halls near the children's areas. I've seen this work well and be a good deterrent. Stop and talk with anyone who does not have a reason to be in the area. I used to tell my team the same thing. I like when I see ushers with radios and earpieces. I can't tell you what a deterrent an earpiece is. A two-way radio also allows for communication between the team and alerts all if there is an emergency.

I remember one time a recovering alcoholic that I'd been counseling came to church drunk. One of his problems was that he was prone to violence and getting into fights when he was under the influence. He came up to me to talk before the service and apologized for falling off the wagon. He reeked of alcohol and wasn't making much sense when he talked with me. As soon as he went inside the auditorium, I went to each and every usher and security team member. We stood in the back of the room and I pointed the guy out to them. I told them to keep an eye on him and stop him if he made a move toward the stage. I had a military guy that had just returned from Iraq and was fit and ready to tackle him to the ground if he rushed the stage. Thankfully, the guy just sang and listened and left in peace, but this is what I'm talking about—making your ushers sensitive to what's going on. They need to have their antennas up the whole time they're serving and be ready to help when needed.

When I was growing up, I remember my dad was a member of the parking lot patrol team. He roamed our church's two big parking lots during services and looked out for thieves. We had numerous times when people broke into the choir ladies' pocketbooks during the service and cars in the parking lot that were broken into. My dad rotated on this team that was there to deter that from happening. Ushers can also be a great presence as people exit to their vehicles. This is especially comforting and needed at night.

As I said before, I think we often oversimplify roles in the church. We tell ushers to stand in place and pass out bulletins. We tell parking lot attendants to point to parking spaces. No wonder no one wants to serve in these roles. They're boring and meaningless. We need to cast a better vision and get these key roles involved in the security and safety of the church. That's something that people can get behind and support. Books on church security go into great detail on security systems, which is another issue all-together and not something I usually mess with when I do a secret shopper visit. Though I did set off a silent alarm at a church one time and almost got arrested. That's a story for another day.

> ""But he who listens to me shall live
> securely and will be at ease from the
> dread of evil." – Proverbs 1:33 (NASB)

You should install alarm systems to deter intruders. While a security system may not stop a break-in, they can be a great deterrent. Also, if someone does break-in, people on the call list get notified and know to go check it out. The police also get notified and come check it out. I strongly urge you to install a security system at your church, regardless of church size. Welch writes about installing a security camera system as a deterrent, "While cameras do not completely stop crime, their presence does serve as a deterrent."[29]

The latest tragedy that comes to mind happened in my home state of South Carolina. The Charleston church shooting was a mass shooting that took place at the Emanuel African Methodist Episcopal Church in downtown Charleston, South Carolina on the evening of June 17, 2015. During a prayer service, nine people were killed by a gunman, including the senior pastor, state senator Clementa C. Pinckney. A tenth victim survived. The morning after the attack, police arrested a suspect, later identified as 21-year-old Dylann Roof, in Shelby, North Carolina.

Do you remember how they caught Dylann Roof? It was from that still frame from the church's video security camera. Cameras matter, friends. After that shooting, we installed all new video cameras that linked to a security office in my home church. We had someone constantly monitoring these cameras during our service and communicating with a security team member standing in the back of the auditorium via radios.

So, what do I look for when I do a secret shopper visit? I look for uniformed police officers. I look for plain-clothed police officers. I look for ushers and security team members with earpieces in their ear. I look for video cameras and locked doors. Any kinds of deterrents that are in place for me not to wander around and go places that I shouldn't be able to go (and trust me, I do try to go where I'm not supposed to go). I look for someone to stop me from wandering, look me square in the eye and say, "May I help you?"

If I could sum up this entire chapter on security, it's all about deterring people with ill intent. If someone wants to break into your church, steal something from your church or God-forbid, go on a shooting rampage, there's a good chance they'll try. Good security in the local church is about deterring things like that from happening. It's about making someone think twice: "Do I really want to go through with this?" or "That man looks like he'll shoot me or taze me." or "I don't think I can get away with this without getting caught." That's the whole point. Make them think twice. Make it difficult to get away with anything bad happening at your church and to your congregation. People deserve to worship in peace and safety and it's your job to help provide that peace.

8

THE WORSHIP SERVICE EXPERIENCE

"Without worship, we go about miserable."
—A. W. Tozer

"If someone doesn't have much use for
praising Him now, it's foolish to think
they're ready for heaven." —Matt Chandler

After looking at all the items in the previous chapters, I will make my way into the worship service. Now there are several things I look for when I do this, starting with the pre-service vibe and atmosphere. Is there appropriate music playing pre-service that sets the tone and feeling for the day? Are there pre-service slides with announcements and welcoming visuals playing on the screens? Is the stage clear and looking nice and neat?

By the way, there's nothing worse than walking into a service before it begins and having to sit through the worship team finishing up their rehearsal. It ruins the whole experience. People don't want to see or hear that. The stage should be clear of all musicians and it's a nice touch to have a warm lighting look on the stage, with the lights over the congregation dim and inviting.

If you want a rule or guide to give your worship team, they should wrap up rehearsal and exit the stage thirty minutes before the first service. If your first service starts at 9:30am, the doors should be open at 9:00am with a clear stage, announcement slides running on the screens, and a pre-service set of music playing overhead. Churches that go to the next level create special playlists on iTunes or Spotify each week that have songs relevant to the theme of the day.

Once I find my seat, I start looking through the bulletin or worship guide that I was handed as I walked in. A bulletin can say a lot about a church. I'm not saying you have to have expensive, multi-colored bulletins. I'm saying what you put in your bulletin says a lot about your church and what you consider important. If your bulletin is busy with numerous announcements and activities listed, you can intimidate a newcomer.

Another thing I look for when I visit or consult with a church is some type of connection card or communication card. This can be perforated and tear off from your bulletin, or simply an insert in the bulletin that people see. Some churches put these on the backs of seats (in pockets) or on the chairs. You need some way for your people (and guests especially) to communicate with your pastoral staff. I always like to call attention to the connection card in the service and encourage first and second-time guests to fill them out and turn them in the offering basket.

Please note: The connection card is all we ask from our guests. We don't expect them to give money when they're visiting. You shouldn't either. Make them feel at ease and say, "When you see the offering basket come by, that's for our regular members and attenders. All we ask from you is to fill out the connection card and put it in the basket so we can send you some information about the church. Thanks so much!" Speaking of the offering, churches handle this in various ways. Some churches (like my last church) don't collect an offering. They have offering baskets in the back of the auditorium where people can turn in their offering and connection cards. Some churches (like my current church) actually pass a plate or basket each week.

There's no right or wrong way to do this. I've seen both be effective and know churches that do it both ways. On a side note, more and more churches are going to digital or online giving (as their primary push) and I'd encourage your leadership to keep this before your congregation. As I said in the Introduction, I love missional churches and communities, but this book is for the majority of churches in North America that embrace an attractional model of ministry and encourage their people to invite friends and family to a Sunday service.

I know there's a lot of discussion and debate about whether a church should be attractional or missional. I've talked extensively about it all over the country. I'm a both/and person and like for a church to seek to be both, but when it comes to the corporate worship service I look for an attractional model. Again: COMPEL them to come in. Blow your community away with excellence and an environment that allows the Holy Spirit of God to move.

"We are called not simply to communicate
the gospel to nonbelievers; we must
also intentionally celebrate the gospel
before them." —Timothy Keller

I never got over Sally Morgenthaler's book *Worship Evange-lism.* I think lost people can be moved by witnessing genuine and authentic worship. I also know God moves through the preaching of His word. Please know I'm not talking to just large churches. I work with several small churches. They do things with excellence and for a small church, really impress me. Regardless of what size church you have, you should think through worship flow, song selection, authenticity, communication/preaching, and every aspect of what you want people to experience each week when you gather. Is sound, video, and lighting important? I think so, but you don't have to have the best of the best to see God move. Whether you're in a school, movie theater, gym, or worship center, you can seek to create an environment where people encounter the Living God.

Many churches I respect and keep an eye on aren't showy or flashy. There are no moving lights and smoke—just genuine, heartfelt music that lifts up the name of Jesus. Some churches are produced and that's fine. Like I said before, "It takes all kinds of churches to reach all kinds of people." Just be yourself and do whatever works best to reach your community.

Whether you're singing music with a pipe organ accompaniment, a choir, a praise team, or band, you should seek to engage in passionate, meaningful, Spirit-filled worship. It should be your goal to lead people into the presence of God, not put on a show. I'm passionate about interactive, engaging, participatory worship. When you gather corporately, it should be an experience of joy, reflection, prayer, teaching the Word, and congregational singing.

I was glad when they said to me, "Let us go into the house of the Lord." – Psalm 122:1 (NKJV)

Also, whether your church is a traditional church, blended church, or modern worship church, you should strive for excellence in all you do. I have secret shopped Churches of Christ that sing without instruments. I have worked with traditional churches that just use piano and organ, or orchestra. I've also worked with modern worship churches that utilize a full rock band and sound, video and lights. Regardless of your musical style, there is no excuse for being unprepared, sloppy, or having moments of awkwardness.

What do I mean by this? If you're going to lead worship, do it well and thoughtfully. Put some effort into it. I don't mean turn it into a show or production. I mean lead with excellence. Work on transitions and think through your song selection. I've secret shopped a variety of churches, different in size, style, and denominations, but the one thing that transcends them all is the value of excellence. As Psalm 33:3 reads, "Play skillfully."

One huge pet peeve of mine is worship leaders that use music stands. This is a visible barrier to connecting with your congregation and is a distraction to the worshiper. They don't want to see you looking down at a music stand. They want to see you confidently lead them in song. Pastors, you should require this from your choir, the worship leader, and the praise team singers. If they don't know the songs well enough to lead them from memory, they shouldn't be on the stage leading. And yes, I'm fine with confidence monitors or prompt screens in the back of the auditorium, as long as their eyes are not glued to them.

At every church that I secret shop, I look for what I call a "God-moment," a time when the Spirit of God moves so powerfully that I stop evaluating and observing and join in and worship. These God-moments come from worship teams that are prepared, intentional, and strategic. If your transitions are sloppy, your musicians are unprepared, and your singers are glued to their music stands, don't expect a God-moment to happen often. Yes, God can move as He pleases, but He tends to show up in powerful ways when we give Him our best and take our roles seriously.

I remember years ago hearing Bill Hybels coach younger pastors like Craig Groeschel and others to incorporate more diversity in their worship team. It's important to think through whom you allow to lead worship. Besides their ethnicity, what impression do they give to the congregation? Are they engaging and encouraging others as they sing? Do they look like they're dead or at a funeral? Trust me. I've seen it, and it's not pretty. I do encourage churches to have an audition process and filter out worship team members that would be a negative distraction to your church's worship. You can find out a lot about someone from an audition.

Another thing I listen for when I'm in the worship service is the overall sound. I check the sound level with a dB (decibel) meter app on my iPhone. Most churches shoot for between 90-95 dB (A weighted). If you're over 95 dB, you don't want to go there for too long. You can do some damage to your people's ears. I would shoot for right around 90 dB. It's important to go for an overall good mix. This requires training on the part of your audio mixer or sound engineer. It's a good investment to make to get them training and to understand that they're not just pushing knobs and buttons. They are helping usher people into the presence of God. A bad mix can be distracting.

A few more things that I evaluate when I do a secret shopper visit are the lyrics on the screen and the use of the screen in general, the sermon/preacher, and how the response is done at the end of the service. Let me explain each briefly. As far as the screen(s) in your auditorium, you need to think through what you display on them, how it is displayed and how it looks to a guest. Make sure your text or lyrics are readable. I once got into a disagreement with someone who wanted to make the lyrics super small, and the people in the back of the auditorium couldn't read it. He wanted it to look cool and wasn't practical enough to realize that if they can't read it, they can't participate and sing along. Don't go too big with your lyrics either. That's just an eye soar. I'd also encourage you to stay away from cheesy pictures and graphics that are outdated. Get a designer or someone with a good eye for design to create your announcement slides.

Some of the most powerful moments in a worship experience are when the screen goes dark. It doesn't always have to be full of images and motion. Don't be afraid to use still backgrounds. Overdoing it with motion backgrounds can be overwhelming to the eyes and over-stimulating. People will leave with a headache and not know why.

Next, I always try to be an encourager to the pastor/preacher, but I do give constructive feedback and take extensive notes during his sermon. One thing I look for is his teaching style (is he conversational and engaging or does it seem like I'm sitting in a classroom). Another thing I look for is for him to teach something relevant to my life. Yes, preach the gospel. Absolutely. But preach in a way that brings about life change. This is what my friend Billy Hornsby was all about. Billy is the one I dedicated this book to. Billy Hornsby was the President of the ARC Church Planters Network before his passing. Greg Surratt, who is the Lead Pastor of Seacoast Church, is now the President of ARC, and is big on life-giving churches. Have you ever been in a life-sucking church? Ha! Life-giving is the opposite of that.

The reason I love my friends at ARC is because from the beginning of their organization, they have sought to bring life, joy, excitement, generosity, and compassion back to the local church. God help us if we ever make church boring or a chore. Seek to lead a life-giving church. I could talk at length about sermons and sermon delivery, but I'll just wrap it up with this. Give your people a word that edifies and guides them. Seek to be practical. Not self-help, but teaching that actually matters to your congregation on Monday and Tuesday. You should always be able to answer the question: "So what?" to each of your messages. What do you want your people to take away from the sermon and how are they to live it out?

This all leads to the end of the message. What do you want the response to be? Are you going to end in prayer? Have an invitation to the gospel? Offer a call for people to rededicate their lives? Lead a call for people to raise hands in response or come forward? All this needs to be carefully thought out and prayed over each week. Start your planning with the end game in mind. Be intentional with where you want your service to go and how you want your people to respond. I pray you have amazing experiences of corporate worship in your congregation.

9
KEEPING IT REAL

This chapter is not only about what I look for when I visit a church or consult with a church. This chapter is what your guests look for. One thing that is crucial today, not only with Millennials, but with people in general, is a realness and authenticity with the church, its leaders and its congregation. People want you to be genuine. Can you blame them? Brian Coffey, senior pastor at First Baptist Church East in Geneva, Illinois, and himself the father of four Millennials, agrees, "Millennials don't like to be programmed to. They can hear honesty. They have a radar for that."[30]

Now, please know, I don't think there's anything wrong with trying to be relevant. I think we must contextualize the gospel. However, I agree that we must be real as well. I could name several churches that I've experienced that were extremely relevant, but did not come across as real and the pastor seemed fake, insincere, aloof, inaccessible, or like an untouchable rock star. No one wants to experience that.

When I secret shop or visit a church, I always stick around after the service is over and see if I can find the senior pastor. I look to see if he is available, accessible, and interacting with people. This accessibility goes a long way toward making a good first impression for guests that may want to meet the pastor for the first time. I think accessibility of the senior pastor is another subtle and powerful statement of a church. Even some of the pastors of the largest churches in America make an intentional and strategic effort to be seen, greeted, and hugged after a service. They may have a bodyguard present for security reasons, but they are available and willing to pray with people that need to speak to their pastor.

Some churches have a designated "Guest Central," like Steve Stroope at Lake Pointe in Rockwall, TX or Brady Boyd at New Life in Colorado Springs. Some have a "Meet and Greet" or VIP Room". Some pastors stand down at the altar and meet and pray with people like Kevin Myers at 12Stone in Atlanta. Some walk around the campus shaking hands like Don Wilson at Christ's Church of the Valley in Phoenix. Erwin McManus at Mosaic LA has an "After Party," where the pastor is present and available to meet with newcomers. This, especially in a large church, goes a long way toward countering the rock star or unavailable pastor stigma that so many guests walk into the church expecting.

Another component of keeping it real is your people's friendliness. Now I'll admit, this is a tough thing to carry out. When I consult with a church, I also write about how friendly the people were. Not only to me, but to each other. Do they stick around after the service is over and socialize? Do they rush out of the building? Are they a real community or just people taking up pews each week? I rate this and evaluate this when I visit a church, but I always say this is one of those intangible qualities that a church either has or doesn't have. You don't want to stand behind the pulpit each week and exhort your people to smile and shake hands with those around them. You will come across as forcing the issue.

However, I think this goes back to the leadership and the senior pastor being real. At my church, I've seen my pastor down front in the auditorium talking and praying with people. When I was on staff at Transformation Church, I saw Derwin Gray outside in the parking lot after a service, giving people high-fives and hugs as they exited the building. He's as real and likable off the stage as he is on the stage.

Gary McIntosh writes,

> "If you were to survey churches and ask them to list their strengths, almost every one would include, 'We're a friendly church.' I know this for a fact as I have asked this question of more than one thousand churches during the last twenty-five years. It's interesting that in every one of the churches I coached, someone either wrote on a survey or stated verbally that they believed their church to be a friendly place. It did not matter if the individuals were attending churches in danger of closing down, in the midst of twenty-year-long plateaus, or bursting forth in growth. They all felt their church was a friendly one. Apparently, regardless of the state of their health or their size, most churches consider themselves to be friendly.
>
> However, if you were to have surveyed the visitors who attended those same churches, you might have been given an opposite perception. For example, in one church I consulted with a few years ago, I discovered

that during a two-year period only 3 visitors out of 197 had chosen to remain in the church. Apparently, more than 97 percent of that church's visitors did not feel welcomed."[31]

You wouldn't believe how many newcomers feel that the church they visited is unwelcoming or unfriendly. I've been to churches where no one spoke to me. I always look for how many people greet me and each other. Do people in the congregation socialize after the service or run for the door? We all know or have heard that perception is reality. It doesn't matter if you grew up in the church or have been on staff for 20 years. If you're neighbor or co-worker doesn't feel welcomed, your church isn't friendly. I wrote this book to help you break down those walls and barriers.

Perception is reality, so what is my advice? Create a culture of friendliness, generosity, grace, hope, and love. Smile. No, really. Smile. Smile often. When you meet with your servant leaders, remind them of why they do what they do and whom we're trying to reach. Shower them with love. At Transformation Church, one of their values is People over Production: "We are committed, by the Spirit's enabling power, to value people for more than what they can produce. We will not prostitute people over and against their spiritual health and transformation."[32]

When your congregation, leaders, and volunteers feel loved, valued, and cared for, it's not only right and proper, it makes a difference in how they serve, give, and take ownership in the vision. When the entire church is on mission together, it's a beautiful thing and guests pick up on it. They may not be able to verbalize what they're experiencing, but they are in a grace atmosphere and it has an impact.

Remember, this book is all about removing distractions. Servants that look like they're tired, bored, disinterested, or not engaged send the wrong message to your guests. It's like they are screaming with their face, "Get out while you can!" When people are valued and loved by the leadership, they're happy to gather together and it shows. So, to wrap this chapter up: Love well. Shower people with grace. Value people over production. Be real, even more than you are relevant. Stick around and talk with people before and after each service. And lastly, smile.

10
FINISH STRONG

I have fought the good fight, I have
finished the race, and I have remained
faithful. – 2 Timothy 4:7 (NLT)

Often when one thinks of a first impression, you may think about the first few moments of the visit. And yes, you have ten minutes to make a huge first impression, but a first impression of a church lasts the entire week after the initial visit. You should finish strong the day of the visit and you should follow-up with guests the week after the visit. It's simply not enough for greeters and parking lot attendants to say "Hello" or "Welcome" when one walks into their church. To go to another level, have your Guest Services or Hospitality team stationed at their posts when the service ends to say

"Goodbye" or "Have a nice week". This goes a long way to wrapping a bow around the entire morning experience and will send them off with a lasting positive impression.

This is something that I look for every time I do a secret shopper visit. Your church's greeters, First Impressions Team, and Parking Lot Team should not disappear after they serve before the service (this happens the majority of the time). No, they should be present and active after the service is over. I like to see the Welcome Center with people ready to serve before *and* after the service. I like to see greeters holding the doors open for me as I exit saying, "Have a great week!" I like to see parking lot attendants smiling and waving goodbye, as well as directing traffic. You don't want your last impression of your church to be like leaving a professional sports game. Take the tension out of a crowded parking lot by helping people as they leave your church.

Recently I secret shopped a restaurant, and the company that hired me wanted to make sure that I was greeted warmly as my wife and I entered and that we were told, "Thank you for coming!" as we left. This goes a long way and those in the hospitality and guest services industry know this. Your church's first impression continues throughout the week following a guest's visit. They may not be expecting anything from you, but a nice follow-up will come as a pleasant surprise to most newcomers. I like to receive a letter or card in the mail when I visit somewhere. My kids have even received nice hand-written cards and notes from the children's minister after visiting a church for the first time.

How do we get guests to return and become fully-engaged? Well, I am a big proponent of the Communication Card (having people fill out some sort of response or communication card), so we can gather data, allow people to sign up, let us know if they are guests, and various other uses. On our Communication Card, there's a place for you to check off if you're a first-time guest or second-time guest. We contact both (this is important).

My admin goes through the Communication Cards on Monday and gives me a list of all first and second-time guests. For the first-time guests, I write a handwritten thank you note to thank them for coming and encourage them to come back. Inside the note, we give them a $5 gift card to Subway. I also have a first-time guest email that goes out to anyone that included their email on their Communication Card. If they included their phone number, I also try to call them at some point later in the week to see if they have any questions about our church and again encourage them to come back the following Sunday. Why is all this contact with first-time guests so important? Searcy says it best:

> "When your guests return for a second look, you've won 80 percent of the battle of gaining new regular attenders and have increased the chances they'll begin a journey with Christ. Their return signals a new level of interest and openness that is very exciting.
>
> When your guests hit the door for the second time, they are saying, 'Okay, I'm interested. I want to find out more about this place. I want to find out more about God. Here I am again. Let's see where this goes.'"[33]

Did you catch that? If your guests return for a second visit, you've won 80% of the battle, and they are much more likely to make a decision for Christ! Wow! So, we put everything into getting first-time guests to become second-time guests. You could say this is why I wrote this book. I want your first-time guests to turn into second-time guests, and I want to see them begin a relationship with Christ.

What do we do for second-time guests? For our second-times guests (that check-off that box on our Communication Card), I send a form letter that is geared to a returning guest and I talk about next steps (like getting plugged into a small group or checking out our newcomer's class). In the letter and envelope is another $5 gift card, but this time the card is to Sonic. I also have a second-time guest email that I send to them, which outlines next steps and encourages them to begin to get plugged in.

Assimilation is an often overlooked or under-appreciated part of church ministry. It is vital to closing the back door to your church and helping your ministry grow. Another key that I want to help highlight is how crucial it is to get people plugged in. If people can get plugged into a small group and/or begin to serve in some area of ministry, they are going to naturally be assimilated into our church and chances are, they will stick around. When I was a Campus Pastor at a multi-site church, I took my staff on a retreat. We brainstormed, dreamed, and prayed for hours. We wanted to come up with what it was we wanted our people to do.

After much time in discussion, I said I think for us, the win is for people to take their next step, whatever that may be.

For some the next step may be salvation or crossing the line of faith. For some the next step may be getting baptized. For some the next step may be joining a small group. For some the next step may be leading or hosting a small group. For some the next step may be signing up to serve. For some the next step may be church membership. For some the next step may be going on a short-term mission trip. You get the picture.

We wanted to offer easy on-ramps and ways for people to assimilate into the body. From the newcomer to the long-time attender or member, we wanted them to be able to take their next step and to grow spiritually. For my church and my campus, this is what assimilation or incorporation looks like. For Saddleback in California and Church of the Highlands in Birmingham, it's moving from 101 to 201 to 301 to 401. Your church may be totally different. I've seen 3 C's and circles. I've seen linear and non-linear ways to show spiritual growth. You have to get away and pray and brainstorm and see what God is leading your church to do, but please don't let me or this book lead you to think that your job is over once you greet people with terrific guest services and hospitality ministries. Those are crucial, yes, but so is following up with guests and helping them move closer to God and assimilate into the local church body.

This is all a work in progress for me and most churches. I don't have all the answers. I just thought someone could benefit from this and thought I'd share it as a resource to you. I hope it helps. God bless you as you try to be a stickier church and turn your first-time guests into second-time guests, and your second-time guests into fully devoted followers of Christ.

CONCLUSION

"We are what we repeatedly do. Excellence,
then, is not an act, but a habit." - Aristotle

This book can't replace the eyes, ears, nose, and experience of a secret shopper, but it can give you things to look out for and put into place if you don't have the budget to bring one in. My heart for you and your church is that the outside draws you in and the inside drives you out into your community. I pray that God blesses your ministry and you make Jesus famous in your city.

I remember 16 years ago attending the Evangelism Conference at Willow Creek and hearing Bill Hybels attribute the growth of his church to word-of-mouth. Anyone that knows anything about marketing knows that you can't beat word-of-mouth marketing. It's always the best form of marketing.

I once preached a message on partnership to my church in Missouri. I talked about our partnership in the gospel (Philippians 1:5). I said that for us advancing the gospel is all about partnership. We're in this together. I then told people to turn to their neighbor and say, "We're in this together."

Often I think of the words of Peter Drucker, the business guru, who always asked business owners two questions: "What business are you in?" and "How's business?" Great questions. From time to time we need to be reminded what we're all about. If you are a church that's committed to the Great Commandment and the Great Commission, you need to hold that up in front of your people. Remind them why you gather and why you scatter.

In that message I told my church our promise as a staff: We won't embarrass you. We put a lot of thought, work, prayer, and creativity into each and every week. Then I addressed the lost people in attendance and told them we're passionate about loving God and loving people. I wanted them to know that they're accepted and loved. It's not about numbers. Rick Warren likes to say, "We count people because people matter to God." We're excited to grow because it means we're reaching more people with the good news. Perry Noble used to say,

"Every number has a name. Every name has a story. Every story matters to God." I like that!

I'm an evangelist for my favorite Mexican restaurant. The place has excellent food and great customer service. I have a great experience there, and I want to introduce people to them. They don't need to advertise because they have such a great thing going on.

Whether it's the fabulous food at our favorite restaurant, the excitement of a great movie, the luxurious accommodations at our favorite hotel, or the life-changing impact of a church ministry, most of us can't help but tell others when we've been well served. And no one needs to tell us to do so.

Larry Osborne in his book *Sticky Church* writes:

> "Perhaps the most common form of natural evangelism is what I like to call come-and-see evangelism. It takes place whenever someone shares a spiritual need or interest and we respond by inviting him or her to come to a Bible study, or attend a church service, or just to hang out with some of our Christian friends...

> But a sticky church offers the perfect environment for come-and-see evangelism, because while every service is designed to help Christians become better Christians, it is always done in a way that non-Christians can understand everything that's said and takes place.

> That makes it much easier for even the most introverted and reserved among us to say with confidence when a friend or co-worker expresses a spiritual interest or need, 'Why don't you just come and see?'"[34]

I was re-reading Bill Hybel's book *Just Walk Across the Room*. In it he writes, "Life's greatest moments evolve from simple acts of cooperation with God's mysterious promptings—nudges that always lean toward finding what's been lost and freeing what's been enslaved." Later in the book, Bill Hybels writes, "To clear up any confusing His first-century audience might have had about why He came, Christ said, 'I came to seek and to save what was lost.'"[35] That's it! People were Jesus' one thing. And they still are. People who are sick. People who are lonely. People who are wandering, depressed, and hopeless. People who have gotten themselves tangled up in suffocating habits and destructive relationships. Friends, if you have been wrecked by God's gift of new life, and if you want to live your life as an expression of love for the great God you know, then let's crank up our boldness meters and introduce as many people as possible to the God who desperately wants to enfold them in His grace!

On October 23, 2014, Rick Warren posted on social media: "The first job of leadership is to love people. Leadership without love is manipulation." Yes! So true. I told you in the Introduction that this was a leadership book. When we love, we lead. When we serve, we lead. There's no such thing as just plain leadership. It's all servant leadership. Love your people well. Be sure they know they are more than just a volunteer or pew-warmer. Encourage your people. Cast vision. Coach. Train. Shepherd. It takes a lot of dedicated people to create a welcoming atmosphere at the typical church. Make sure you remind your people why they do what they do and whom you're trying to reach.

Many churches have regular leadership development meetings for their servant leaders. You must constantly love, encourage, cast vision, train, and equip. Remind your people what it is like when someone walks through the church doors for the first time. Always be empathetic to guests and the importance of removing distractions.

From Mark Waltz's classic book *First Impressions*, he writes: "One final comment about identifying and removing distractions: Put yourself in the position of your guests and anticipate potential problems. Know what could go wrong, then prevent it. Of course, you won't be able to anticipate every distraction, but when you develop a pattern of excellence, your guests will offer grace when a distraction does occur."[36] Great words of wisdom. It's all about removing distractions and striving for excellence.

At Andy Stanley's churches, they give their Guest Services Team a copy of the Disney book *Be Our Guest*, which is a terrific guide for how to do customer service and make people feel loved, served, and appreciated.

"In my organization there is respect
for every individual, and we all have
respect for the public." – Walt Disney

Read that quote from Walt Disney again. Friends, our hospitality ministry is not just a Sunday thing. It's not just something we do before the service starts. No! Think long-term.

We love, care for, and value all people from the first time they walk through our doors until their last time—all the way until their funeral.

We don't do hospitality and guest services ministry simply to grow our church. That's the wrong motivation. We do this because all people are precious in the sight of God and made in His image. Is growth a by-product? Yes, but our hospitality and service should be genuine and filled with love, grace, and compassion. Have you noticed that through this entire book, I've referred to people that visit your church as "guests?" I always cringe when I'm at a church and they say they'd like to welcome any visitors. "Visitor" is a cold term and is outsider lingo.

I always encourage churches that have designated Visitor Parking to change it to Guest Parking. It's a mindset and approach to first impressions that speaks volumes. The way I describe it to churches that I consult is if you were having company over to your home, you would clean up. In the same way, we have "company" or "guests" each and every week at our churches, and we need to be prepared. We need to clean up (remove distractions and barriers) and take what we do seriously. This book is ultimately about excellence and doing what you do well. You will never get a second chance to make a first impression, so make each Sunday count.

I pray God's greatest blessing upon you, your church, and the ministry that radiates out from your place of service. I pray God uses something in this book to open your eyes to the wonderful opportunity that lies before us, to reach our cities for Christ. And please know: We're in this together! It's all about the Kingdom and I just want to see your church shine and represent Christ and the gospel well. I want to see your church thrive! God bless you as you serve our great and good God.

NOTES

1. Stanley, Andy. *Deep & Wide: Creating Churches Unchurched People Love to Attend*, pp. 16-17.

2. Hirsch, Alan. *The Forgotten Ways*, p. 45.

3. Reed, Ben. *Starting Small: The Ultimate Small Group Blueprint*, Kindle Locations 154-156.

4. Surratt, Geoff. *The Effective Church*, Kindle Locations 281-282.

5. Stanley, Andy. *Deep & Wide: Creating Churches Unchurched People Love to Attend*, p. 210.

6. Seaver, Bill. "The Two Things Needed to Change Your Marketing." *MicroExplosion*. Bill Seaver, 7 Jan. 2009. Accessed online: 27 May 2016.

7. Smith, Nils. "Developing a Facebook Content Strategy." Nils Smith Solutions, 17 Feb. 2016. Accessed online: 27 May 2016.

8. Meacham, Jon. "Preach Like Your Faith Depends on It." *TIME Magazine* 25 Mar. 2013. Accessed online: 27 May 2016.

SECRETS OF A SECRET SHOPPER

9. World Internet Users Statistics and 2015 World Population Stats." *World Internet Users Statistics and 2015 World Population Stats.* INTERNET USAGE STATISTICS, 27 May 2016. Accessed online: 27 May 2016.

10. "7 Most Visited Church Website Pages." *Collide Magazine* 1 July 2010. Accessed online: 27 May 2016.

11. https://adata.org/factsheet/parking

12. Ibid.

13. Stevens, Tim. "Leading Smart." Stevens, 1 July 2010. Accessed online: 27 May 2016.

14. Waltz, Mark L. *First Impressions: Creating Wow Experiences in Your Church.* Loveland, CO: Group Pub., 2005.

15. Ibid.

16. Reiland, Dan. *Usher Training Manual.* Lawrenceville: 12Stone Church, 5 Sept. 2008.

17. Trent, Michael. "Leading from Behind the Bar." *GregAtkinson.com.* Greg Atkinson, 21 May 2014. Accessed online: 27 May 2016.

18. Batterson, Mark. "Postmodern Wells: Creating a Third Place." *MarkBatterson.com.* Mark Batterson, 23 May 2006. Accessed online: 27 May 2016.

19. Atkinson, Greg. *Keep Them Coming: Ideas for Closing the Back Door of Your Church.* ChurchLeaders.com ebook.

20. Surratt, Geoff. *The Effective Church.* 1 Jan. 2014. Kindle

Locations 223-250.

21. Fogg, Steve. "8 Steps to Making Interior Signs Work for Your Church." Church Marketing Sucks, 26 June 2013. Accessed online: 27 May 2016.

22. Ibid.

23. Ibid.

24. Surratt, Geoff. *The Effective Church.* 1 Jan. 2014. Kindle Locations 223-250. Used with permission.

25. Stevens, Tim. "Three Growth Lids." 10 Jan. 2009. Accessed online: 27 May 2016.

26. Welch, Robert H. *Serving by Safeguarding Your Church.* Grand Rapids, MI: Zondervan, 2002.

27. Ibid.

28. Ibid.

29. Ibid.

30. Liautaud, Marian V. "5 Things Millennials Wish the Church Would Be." Exponential, 15 Oct. 2014. Accessed online: 27 May 2016.

31. McIntosh, Gary. *Beyond the First Visit: The Complete Guide to Connecting Guests to Your Church.* Grand Rapids, MI: Baker, 2006. Kindle Locations 172-192

32. Gray, Derwin L. "New Here?" Transformation Church website. Accessed online: 27 May 2016.

33. Searcy, Nelson, and Jennifer Dykes Henson. *Fusion:*

Turning First-time Guests into Fully Engaged Members of Your Church. Ventura, CA: Regal, 2007.

34. Osborne, Larry W. *Sticky Church.* Grand Rapids, MI: Zondervan, 2008.

35. Hybels, Bill. *Just Walk across the Room: Simple Steps Pointing People to Faith.* Grand Rapids, MI: Zondervan, 2006.

36. Waltz, Mark L. *First Impressions: Creating Wow Experiences in Your Church.* Loveland, CO: Group Pub., 2005.

48263927R00094

Made in the USA
San Bernardino, CA
20 April 2017